INCREDIBLE
BUGS

INCREDIBLE
BUGS

THE ULTIMATE GUIDE TO THE WORLD OF INSECTS

By Rick Imes

Consultant Editors
Steve & Jane Parker

BARNES
&NOBLE
BOOKS
NEW YORK

A QUARTO BOOK

This edition published
by Barnes & Noble, Inc.,
by arrangement with Quarto Inc.

1997 Barnes & Noble Books

ISBN 0-7607-0071-0
M 10 9 8 7 6 5 4 3 2 1

This book was designed and produced by
Quarto Publishing plc
The Old Brewery
6 Blundell Street
London N7 9BH

Senior art editor Elizabeth Healey
Designer Sheila Volpe
Editors Sarah Fergusson, Jo Fletcher-Watson,
Jane Hurd-Cosgrave
Text editor Maggi McCormick
Managing editor Sally MacEachern
Illustrators Elisabeth Smith, Tim Hayward,
Colin Newman, Bob Brampton, Wayne Ford,
Yanos Maffry, Dave Kemp
Picture researcher Miriam Hyman
Picture research manager Giulia Hetherington
Art director Moira Clinch
Assistant art director Penny Cobb
Editorial director Mark Dartford

Typeset in Britain by Type Technique, London

Manufactured in Malaysia
by C H Colour Scan Sdn. Bhd.

Printed in Singapore
by Star Standard Industries (Pte) Ltd

Contents

*A brightly
colored bug
from the Costa
Rican rainforest.*

Introduction

Below

A greenfly aphid with her young. Because of their relatively short life spans, insects enjoy a high reproductive rate.

Who really rules the earth? Being self-centered, we humans would assert that we do. After all, we are obviously the most intellectually advanced species.

Indeed, superficially, we have all the hallmarks of a supremely powerful life form; we might even appear god-like to lower species, if they have any concept of "God." However, before we declare ourselves the ultimate biological product, let's examine the evidence.

Humans are a mere 4 million years old, compared with the Earth's age of 4.6 billion years. Our mammalian ancestors have been around considerably longer – approximately 200 million years –

but did not achieve any prominence until mass extinctions swept dinosaurs into oblivion. Size and intelligence, however, do not count for everything – consider what I believe to be our chief rivals: insects.

One scientist estimated that 12,0000 species live in a hectare of rainforest canopy – and that's just beetles!

Insects have been around for nearly 400 million years. There are roughly 1 million species known, and very likely two or three times as many that are as yet unclassified. Compensating for their relatively short life spans and ecological roles as prey, insects enjoy a high rate of reproduction and a correspondingly high incidence of genetic mutations, from which a species draws advantageous traits. It's a case of survival of the fittest: those best able to survive will live to pass on more beneficial traits to offspring than will lesser-endowed individuals.

From an evolutionary standpoint, insects adapt to changes in their environment quite rapidly. Every environmental fluctuation presents opportunities as well as challenges, and there is always an insect species, or mutant within a species, poised to seize

every new opportunity. Coupled with their relatively small size, awesome numbers, incredible diversity, waterproof armor, highly developed senses, and gift of flight, the potential of insects not only to survive but to thrive is simply astounding, and surely outdoes that of every other creature – including humans!

A honeybee grub, fed on nutritious pollen, increases its weight by 1,500 times in 5 days.

Insects are some of the most fascinating creatures on earth. It is only because of their size that we deem them unremarkable. And it is because we humans tend to bond with creatures that are most like us – warm, fuzzy puppies,

bunnies and fawns, or animals of higher intelligence, such as apes and dolphins – that we dismiss insects as being inferior. In addition, we are inclined to be prejudiced against many insects because some species cause damage to our crops, spread disease and inflict painful stings.

This book is intended to make you look at insects in a new light. It is packed with a wealth of amazing information. The facts highlighted here are just to whet your appetite – as you turn the pages you will find more and more reason to appreciate this extraordinary group of animals – the incredible bugs!

Rick Imes

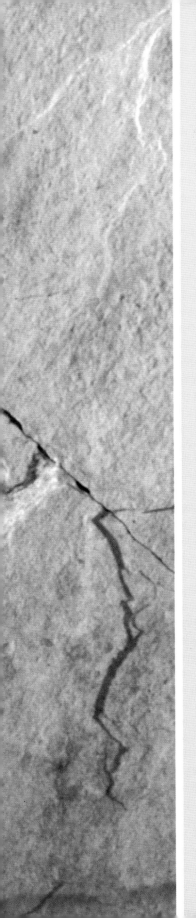

1

INSECT EVOLUTION AND DEVELOPMENT

THE HISTORY OF EVOLUTION IS RECORDED IN FOSSILIZED STONE BUT AS FAR AS INSECTS ARE CONCERNED, THE FOSSIL EVIDENCE IS FAR FROM COMPLETE, LEAVING MUCH ROOM FOR SPECULATION AS TO THEIR TRUE ORIGINS.

TODAY, INSECTS ARE CLASSIFIED WITHIN A LARGER GROUP CALLED ARTHROPODS — SEGMENTED CREATURES WITH HARD, OUTER-BODY CASINGS AND JOINTED LEGS — WHICH ALSO INCLUDES ARACHNIDS, MYRIAPODS, CRUSTACEANS, AND TRILOBITES. BUT WITHIN THE INSECT GROUP ALONE, THERE ARE MANY DIFFERENT SUBGROUPS AND CATEGORIES, AND OVER A MILLION DIFFERENT TYPES OR SPECIES.

INSECTS VARY FROM BEING VERY SMALL TO VERY LARGE (COMPARATIVELY), WINGED TO WINGLESS, FAST TO SLOW, JUMPING TO CRAWLING, AND LIVING UNDERWATER TO BURROWING DEEP IN THE EARTH. THIS AMAZING DIVERSITY AND RANGE OF BUGS IS THE RESULT OF THEIR EVOLUTION OVER MILLIONS OF YEARS TO ADAPT TO DIFFERENT ENVIRONMENTAL CONDITIONS, FOR REPRODUCTIVE PURPOSES, AND FOR DEFENSE AGAINST VARIOUS TYPES OF PREDATORS (INCLUDING OTHER INSECTS). WITH THEIR ADAPTIVE BRILLIANCE AND SHEER TENACITY TO SURVIVE, BUGS ARE TRULY ONE OF THE MOST REMARKABLE "SUCCESS STORIES" OF EVOLUTION.

Insect Evolution and Development

The bodies and behaviors of insects have been shaped by the forces of natural selection over millions of years.

More than 90 percent of all animal species that have evolved during the 3,500 million years of life's history on earth have died out or become extinct. This happened as a result of natural selection, competition for food and resources, and the survival of only the fittest. Because insects form the largest group of animal species alive today, we can only assume that countless millions have appeared, thrived for a time, and are now gone forever.

A history of survival

Insects appeared on earth more than 350 million years before us. Throughout this time, they have been amazingly tough and resilient. They have survived catastrophes of all kinds, such as drought, food, famine, epidemics of disease, and plagues of predators. They'll probably be around long after us.

Above

Silverfish hide by day in cracks and holes. At night they emerge to forage for breadcrumbs and other scraps on the kitchen floor. These wingless creatures were among the first insects, 370 million years ago.

Wings and legs

Most insects have wings and can fly. So they move faster and farther than us. To give you some idea, try following a bee all through a summer's day! Insects have six legs compared to our two. This gives them plenty of scope for using their limbs in many ways – digging, drilling, leaping, running, feeding, swimming, grabbing, and cutting.

Mouths and food

Insect mouth parts can be adapted for chewing, grasping, boring, snipping, sucking, piercing, and lapping. This allows them to deal with and consume a huge variety of foods. Their small body size and special-ized internal chemistry mean they are very efficient at using the nutrients and energy in their meals. And a female insect can produce hundreds, even thousands, of offspring. For most human parents, less than five youngsters is more than enough!

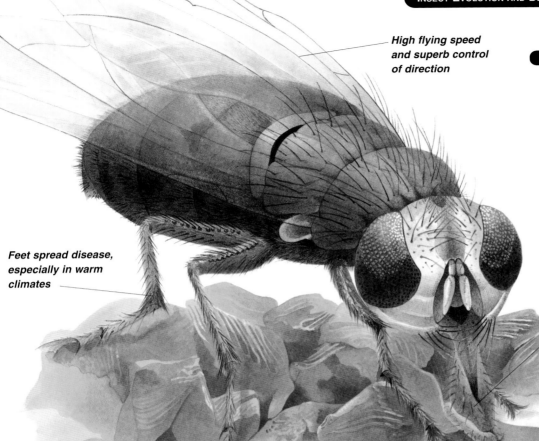

High flying speed and superb control of direction

Feet spread disease, especially in warm climates

Mouthparts extract fluids from decaying material

Left

The ubiquitous housefly was originally a creature of natural grasslands and shrub. But it has adapted, with irritating success, to human habitations.

Adapting to the future

The evolution of living things, as they change through time, depends partly on mutations. These are alterations in the genes which usually crop up randomly and by chance, and alter the living thing in some way. Some mutations are negative and harmful. Others are positive. They cause a new adaptation which helps the organism in some way to survive and reproduce, and thereby pass on the mutated gene.

Insects experience more mutations than other groups of living things. This is due to their sheer abundance in terms of quantities of individuals, plus their huge numbers of offspring, and the speed at which they breed. So insects, when faced with environmental change, are much more likely than other animals to come up with the genetic variations needed to survive. In other words, they are supremely adaptable.

Would you believe?

About 1 million species of insects have been classified. This far exceeds the numbers of all other living species – plants, fungi, and animals – combined. Just one group of insects, the beetles and weevils *(Coleoptera)*, out-numbers all plant species on earth! Biologists guesstimate that there are at least another million insect species still to be discovered; some estimates are above 5 million.

The First Insects

Insect fossils are rare, but we know enough to sketch their ancestry and evolution.

When did insects first appear on earth? Which animals were their ancestors? How have insects changed or evolved through time? Were they alive to pester the dinosaurs? Many of the answers to these questions are guesses, based on the evidence of fossils.

How fossils form
A fossil forms when a plant or animal dies and is quickly covered by sand, silt, or mud. The softer parts of the body usually rot away quickly. But the harder parts are replaced bit by bit by minerals, over thousands and millions of years. Gradually they and the surrounding substance turn to rock.

What becomes fossils?
The bones, teeth, and horns of mammals and reptiles, the skeletons of fish, and the shells of shellfish form good fossils. Insects are small and fairly softbodied, and do not fossilize so well. Many prehistoric insects are known solely by their wings, the only parts tough enough to be preserved. So the fossil record of insect evolution is very incomplete, leaving much room for people to guess and speculate.

Above

Insects that were trapped in tree-bark resin millions of years ago, like these mosquitoes, became fossilized when the sap hardened into amber.

LIFE AND TIME		million years ago
Single-celled animals	**3,000**	
Multicellular creatures	**1,000**	
Segmented worms	**700**	
Velvet Worms	**500**	
Millipedes and centipedes	**400**	

Left
Giant dragonflies as big as crows, with wing spans of 30in (75cm), flitted through the lush, Carboniferous fern forests of 300 million years ago. These were the biggest insects that ever lived.

Insect beginnings

Insects belong to a much bigger animal group called arthropods – segmented creatures with hard, outer-body casings and jointed legs. Arthropods probably evolved from legless, worm-like ancestors, perhaps as revealed by the part-legged velvet worms that still survive today.

But insects were not the first arthropods. This honor may go to the myriapods – the "many-legged" centipedes and millipedes. Fossils indicate that these were the first insect-sized, terrestrial creatures to roam primeval forests of giant ferns, 400 million years ago. Another idea is that insects evolved from crab-like, water-dwelling arthropods called trilobites, which were very common in prehistoric times. One group of trilobites may have taken to life on land, and evolved into insects.

Would you believe?

Cockroaches are perceived as the bane of humankind around the world, yet their original evolutionary design was so successful, they have remained almost completely unchanged for more than 300 million years!

Left
Velvet worms live in damp, tropical forests. They are neither annelids (legless true worms), nor arthropods (joint-legged creatures), but are possibly the "missing link" between these two animal groups.

EARLY INSECTS

Springtails and bristletails 370 million years ago, during the Devonian Period
Cockroaches and dragonflies 345-280 million years ago, during the Carboniferous Period
Beetles, true bugs, and cicadas 280-245 million years ago, during the Permian Period
Flies 190-150 million years ago, during the Jurassic Period
Butterflies 120 million years ago, during the Cretaceous Period
Bees, wasps, and ants 50 million years ago, during the Tertiary Period

Insects as Arthropods

Many creepy crawlies are called "bugs." But there are important differences between insects and other arthropods.

The living world of animals, plants, microbes and other organisms is divided into main groups called phyla (singular: phylum). The biggest of all the phyla is the arthropods. It consists of creatures whose bodies are divided into sections or segments, who have a hard outer body casing called an exoskeleton, and legs that have sections linked by bendy joints (unlike slithery tentacles).

Groups of arthropods

The arthropods include many familiar animals, such as insects, spiders, scorpions, millipedes, crabs, and prawns. These form the various subgroups called classes, which make up the larger phylum. Our everyday word "bug" might refer to all of these classes of arthropods, but usually it is restricted to insects alone. Here are the main living classes of arthropods. Many others, like the trilobites, died out during prehistoric times.

Above

Freshwater crayfish, like many other crustaceans, have large and powerful pincers.

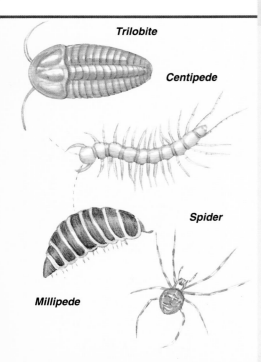

Trilobite

Centipede

Spider

Millipede

ARTHROPODS COMPARED

Trilobites
- Segmented body with two furrows along the back ("three-lobed").
- Head features two eyes, two antennae or feelers, and four pairs of limbs or appendages.
- Body segments have various limbs or other appendages. All extinct.

Chilopoda (centipedes)
- Flattened segmented body with one pair of legs on each segment.
- One pair of poison fangs on the first segment.
- Head with one pair of eyes, one pair of long antennae, and three pairs of mouth parts.

Diplopoda (millipedes)
- Arched, segmented body with two pairs of legs on each segment.
- Head features one pair of eyes, one pair of mouth parts, and one pair of short antennae.

Arachnids (spiders and scorpions)
- Head and thorax joined to make one cephalothorax. This features four pairs of legs and four pairs of mouth parts.
- No antennae.
- Abdomen sometimes segmented.

Xiphosurids (horseshoe crabs)
- Carapace has one pair of compound eyes and six pairs of legs.
- Abdomen is covered by a shield.
- Spear-like tail.

Horseshoe crab

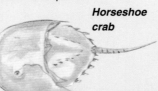

Spiders and kin

The class Arachnida includes spiders, scorpions, ticks, and mites. Scorpions have a pair of formidable pincers, strong mouth parts, and a poisonous sting in the tail. Spiders possess fangs capable of injecting venom, and produce silk from the end of their abdomen.

Centipedes and millipedes (myriapods)

Centipede means "100 feet." Each of the flattened body segments, which vary in number from 15 to more than 180, features one pair of legs. Millipede means "1,000 feet," though few species have more than 200. Each body segment has two pairs of legs. Centipedes are swift hunters with venomous fangs. Millipedes are slow munchers of plants or decaying matter.

Crustaceans

The name comes from the Latin *crusta*, meaning a crust or "hard shell". All crustaceans have an outer-body casing or skeleton. Most, like crabs, lobsters, shrimps, prawns, krill, copepods, and barnacles, live in the sea. Crayfish and water fleas frequent fresh water.

Horseshoe crabs (king crabs)

These "living fossils" have a large, domed, upper-body case or carapace. Behind it, the abdominal shield is armed with spines and a menacing, bayonet-like tail.

Above

Millipedes are scavengers or herbivores. When threatened, their main defenses are to ooze smelly stink-fluids from glands along the body and roll into a tight ball to protect their vulnerable underside.

Crustaceans (crabs, shrimps, and relations)

- Head and thorax joined into a cephalothorax, often covered by a carapace.
- Head features two pairs of antennae, one pair of eyes, and several pairs of mouth parts.
- Various numbers of paired limbs or other appendages (never more than one pair per segment).
- Appendages may be for touch, taste, chewing, food handling, mating, egg carrying, swimming, or circulating water over the gills.
- First pair of limbs sometimes features large, powerful pincers.

Shrimp

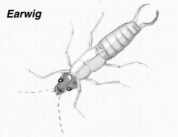

Insects

- Three body divisions of head, thorax, and abdomen.
- Head bears one pair of eyes, one pair of antennae, and several pairs of mouth parts.
- Thorax features two pairs of wings and three pairs of legs.

Earwig

Would you believe?

There are about 1.2 million known species of arthropods. Around 1 million of these are insects! The class Insecta is the biggest of all living things. In contrast, our own class Mammalia (mammals) contains only about 4,000 species.

Grouping Insects

Despite the bewildering variety and diversity of insects, they can be grouped according to bodily features.

A major part of science is grouping and classifying. Bugs have not escaped being organized. Biologists divide the class Insecta into two subclasses. One is insects that do not have wings at any stage in their life cycle; this subclass is called the Apterygota. The other subclass is insects with wings, the Pterygota.

Wingless insects

The Apterygota includes the bristletails, springtails, and silverfish. They are often termed the most primitive insects, partly because they have been around the longest, and partly because their bodies show the least sophistication and modification from the basic insect design. They are tiny and rarely seen, but they are important and abundant recyclers of dead and dying plants, animals, and food matter.

Above

The delicate damselfly has two pairs of similar wings and large compound eyes. It is a territorial hunter, patrolling its patch of stream bank in search of unsuspecting gnats and other prey.

Winged insects

Pterygota is divided into two further groups. In the Exopterygota, the young or offspring are similar in shape and body form to the adults. In the Endopterygota, the young go through marked changes in body shape or form, called metamorphosis, as they grow up to become adults.

Which group for which insect?

How are insects allocated to a group? Usually by a combination of features, including body design and shape, the number and type of wings, and also what happens during the life cycle. Some insects, like the grylloblatids, do not fit neatly with any others. Some biologists force them into an existing group. Others insist on creating a group solely for them. Insect classification is certainly not straightforward!

Naming insects

All living things fit into the two-name or binomial system of biological classification. This was invented by Swedish botanist Carolus Linnaeus and published in 1758.

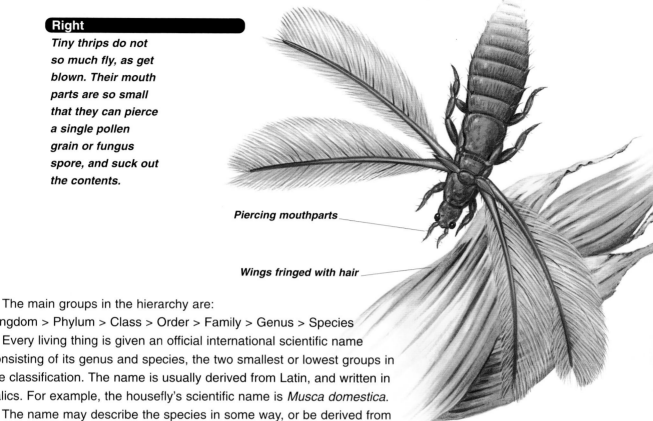

Right

Tiny thrips do not so much fly, as get blown. Their mouth parts are so small that they can pierce a single pollen grain or fungus spore, and suck out the contents.

Piercing mouthparts

Wings fringed with hair

The main groups in the hierarchy are:
Kingdom > Phylum > Class > Order > Family > Genus > Species

Every living thing is given an official international scientific name consisting of its genus and species, the two smallest or lowest groups in the classification. The name is usually derived from Latin, and written in italics. For example, the housefly's scientific name is *Musca domestica*.

The name may describe the species in some way, or be derived from its discoverer's name, or the place it was found.

MAIN INSECTS

There are about 14 sub-subgroups, or orders, of Exopterygota. They include:

Odonata (dragonflies)

Blattodea (cockroaches)

Isoptera (termites)

Hemiptera (true bugs)

Orthoptera (grasshoppers)

The ten or so orders of Endopterygota include:

Hymenoptera (ants, wasps, and bees)

Diptera (flies)

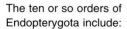
Lepidoptera (butterflies and moths)

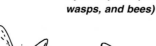
Coleoptera (beetles and weevils)

Where Insects Live

They dwell almost everywhere — from deep in the soil to almost as high as planes can fly!

Insects flourish in almost every habitat on earth, from icy pole to tropical forest, high mountain to mixed woodland, desert to swamp, fast river to still lake, shrubby upland to grassy lowland, and even the seashore. Only the sea remains insect-free – well, not quite.

Insects also abound on every continent, land mass, and major island, except one: Antarctica. The simple reason is lack of food. The ultra-severe climate of Antarctica supports very little plant life; and consequently, only a few species of animals can live there. But, of course, they include insects – springtails and midges.

Where do flies go in the winter?

Insects may seem absent during the winter in temperate lands, such as most of North America, Europe, and Australasia. In fact, they are present in force. But they are dormant, inactive, or sleeping – as millions of eggs, larvae, and pupae (young forms), and adults. They are in cracks, crevices, nooks, soil, crannies, logs, under stones, and in the mud at the bottom of rivers and ponds, awaiting the warmth of spring.

In contrast, most insects of the tropics and subtropics flourish all year round. They can feed on the diversity of plant life that grows continuously in these regions. The world's greatest assortments of insect species are found in the warmth and dampness of the moist tropics.

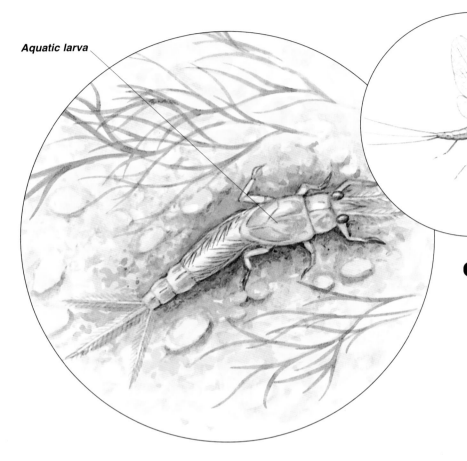

Aquatic larva

Adult

Above

Mayflies spend most of their lives as aquatic larvae (left). They feed on water plants for as long as three years, and then molt into a flying, pre-adult form. The pre-adult then sheds its skin or molts into the adult (above), which lives only a few hours or days.

Insects in fresh water

From a small and temporary puddle to the massive Great Lakes, and from the tiniest mountain stream to the mighty Amazon, insects inhabit every freshwater habitat in the world. They are most diverse in shallow water, where aquatic vegetation is richest. The deeper you go, the fewer insects species you encounter.

Insects in the sea

Insects are conspicuous by their absence in the world's largest habitat – oceans. Only a very few kinds live in salt water. These ocean-dwelling insects include a group of water striders; one or two species of springtails; and some mosquitoes. Perhaps it's just as well that there aren't as many insects there – it might just give other animals a chance!

Many insects live where other creatures could not survive. Certain fly larvae live in hot springs of 140°F (60°C), while snow fleas thrive at -5°F (-15°C). One fly spends its young life covered in crude oil!

Would you believe?

 It is estimated that there are about 67,000 million insects over every square mile of earth. That's about 200 million insects for every human being! We don't notice them because most of them are flying above our heads, burrowing in the ground beneath our feet, or hidden in plants around us.

Large and Small

Insects show tremendous variation in size – greater than almost any other group of living things.

One of the major reasons for insects' unparalleled success is their small size. They can go relatively unnoticed by many larger predators. They are able to enter and invade places that are inaccessible to big animals. They eat foods that are unavailable or uninteresting to larger creatures.

Small and specialized

Small size also allows more individuals to become more specialized and occupy more ecological niches, hence the different roles of various animals and plants in their habitat. Indeed, ecologists would say that many bugs are superspecialized, i.e. fitted to an extremely narrow range of conditions and situations. This creates a huge genetic diversity of small and specialized species. And genetic diversity is always useful as conditions change and evolution occurs.

Below

The beautiful Atlas moths live in Asia, from India and Sri Lanka across to Malaysia, Indonesia, and China. They are the largest of all moths and butterflies.

Lower limit: balls and syrup

However, being little has its drawbacks. As an object becomes smaller, its surface area rises in proportion to its weight. Also, the forces of nature, such as wind and water surface tension, become relatively huge. The tiniest of all insects are the hairy-winged beetles and the fairy flies. To them, the densities of air and water are massive. A fairy fly walking through air is like you pushing through piles of table-tennis balls. And a fairy fly falling into water would be like you sinking into sticky syrup.

Upper limit: suffocation

At the other end of the scale, the insect's heavy body-casing – the exoskeleton – becomes proportionally thicker and heavier, and eventually too weighty for its muscles to move. Also, insects breathe through a network of body tubes called the tracheal respiratory system. This depends on air seeping or diffusing along the tubes. Above a certain size limit, the inner parts of the body are too far from the outside for fresh air to reach them.

MINI-BUGS TO MEGA-BUGS (LIVING SPECIES)

(Typical body length, unless stated)

Hairy-winged beetles
(Trichopterygidae) 0.008 in. (0.2mm) – small enough to crawl through the eye of a sewing needle

Fairy fly
(Mymaridae) 0.02 in. (0.5mm)

Silver water beetle
1¾ in. (45mm) long, and ¾ in. (19mm) wide

Death's-head hawk moth
5⅜ in. (137mm) wingspan

Emperor dragonfly
3 in. (76mm)

Stag beetle
3 in. (76mm), and ¼ oz. (7g) in weight

Cockroach
3¾ in. (86mm) long, and 1¾ in. (45mm) wide

Goliath beetle
(Scarabaeidae) 4⅜ in. (110mm), and 3½ oz. (100g) in weight

Elephant beetle
(*Dynastes*) 6 in. (150mm), and 2½ oz. (70g) in weight

Dragonfly
4¾ in. (120mm), and 7½ in. (190mm) wing span

Queen Alexander's birdwing butterfly
11¼ in. (280mm) wingspan, and 1 oz. (28g) in weight

Great owlet and Atlas moth
12 in. (305mm) wingspan

Stick insects (Palophus titan)
13¼ in. (335mm), 20 in. (500mm) total length, including antennae and legs

---

Would you believe?

Insects are not the largest arthropods. The deep-sea Japanese spider crab has a body the size of a dinner plate, and a span across its outstretched pincers of 3½ yds. (3m). But because it lives in water, this helps to support its weight. On land, without the buoyancy of water, the crab can hardly move.

Three into One

The typical insect has a head to sense and eat, thorax to move, and abdomen to digest and reproduce.

A major feature of the typical adult insect is that its body is divided into three distinct parts. These are the head, thorax, and abdomen. No other major group of animals has this characteristic body structure. However, sometimes the three-part design is obscured by the insect's overall shape, and it is not evident in the immature stages such as larvae and pupae. Also, within the three main body parts, the insect has the basic sectional or segmented body structure as found among other arthropods, worms, and many similar creatures.

At the front

The average bug head is a fairly rigid, capsule-shaped container that encompasses and protects the brain. It bears one pair of antennae or feelers, one pair of compound eyes (with many mosaic-type separate parts), and up to three simple eyes. It also bears the mouth parts, which are numerous and hugely diverse across the insect group. These various head appendages are discussed in detail on pages 48, 60, and 74.

In the middle

Immediately behind the head is the thorax or chest. It has three distinct sections or segments – prothorax, mesothorax, and methathorax. Each of these has a pair of legs attached at the lower, outer corners (the pleura). The mesothorax and metathorax each have a pair of wings joined to the upper, outer corners (tergae). Legs and wings are shown in detail on pages 30-43.

Left

Ants, wasps, and bees have a thin tube – a "wasp waist" – between their thorax and abdomen, through which the main blood vessel, nerve, and intestine pass.

Would you believe?

The sting of a bee, wasp, or ant is a modified egg-laying tube, the ovipositor. It is housed in the last body segment of the abdomen. When a honeybee worker stings in defense of the hive, the sharp, barbed sting and its pulsating venom sac are ripped away and left in the victim, together with other contents from the rear of the bee's abdomen. The bee is mortally wounded.

At the rear

The abdomen is usually the largest body division, and has many segments. It is rounder, softer, and more elastic than the head or thorax, allowing some insects to make breathing movements and draw air into the network of respiratory tubes, the tracheae. These open at holes called spiracles; there is one pair on each segment, but none on the rearmost few segments. The other main visible feature of the abdomen is the reproductive organs, or external genitalia, at the very rear. In many females, this is a prominent egg-laying tube or ovipositor. In males, the genitalia may be extended and visible, or retracted. Digestive leftovers and body wastes are expelled from the anus, a hole above the genitalia.

BODY PARTS

Here are the three main body parts of a typical insect, and the appendages they feature.

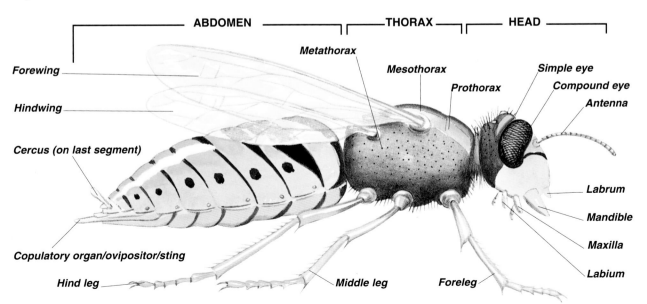

Inside an Insect

An insect has the main organs possessed by most animals – packed into a much smaller body!

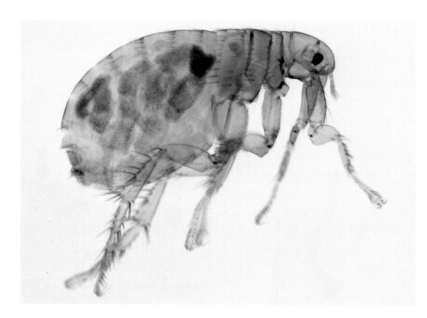

The main parts or organs in an insect's body work together as systems. Each body system carries out one major role in the process of staying alive, such as breathing to obtain oxygen, or digesting food and excreting wastes.

Respiratory system

Insects "breathe" through holes called spiracles along the sides of the thorax and abdomen. Each spiracle leads into a branching network of flexible tubes called tracheae. These divide into even thinner tubes called tracheoles. Air seeps or diffuses in and out of the tubes, carrying vital oxygen to all body tissues.

Above

Most of an insect's life support organs are in its abdomen. In addition to the main intestines visible inside this flea, there are also several muscles, fine branches of nerves, and other, smaller parts.

Circulatory system

Insects have an open circulation. The tube-like heart draws in blood from the general body cavity through valved openings. It pumps this blood – more correctly called hemolymph – towards the head, through the main aorta blood vessel. This divides into smaller vessels that open into the general body cavity. As the blood flows around the organs, it distributes nutrients and removes wastes.

Digestive and excretory systems

An insect does not have an obvious mouth. The digestive tube begins at the head, where salivary glands produce lubricating and digestive juices. Food passes through the pharynx to the esophagus (gullet) and into the crop, a storage bag. Next is the muscular gizzard, where solid material is mashed. Then comes the stomach, containing digestive chemicals called enzymes. Nutrients are distributed into the blood-filled body cavity, both in the stomach and the adjoining region, the intestine.

Body wastes are absorbed from the blood by thread-like malpighian tubules. These empty the wastes into the intestine, to be expelled from the anus, along with the leftovers (feces) from digestion itself.

Nervous system

The insect's brain is inside its upper head. Nerves extend to the sensory organs, especially antennae and eyes, and around the esophagus to a bundle of nerves called a ganglion, which serves the mouth parts. From here, a ventral (underside) nerve cord runs the length of the creature. Each body segment contains a pair of ganglia on this nerve cord, with smaller nerves branching to the wings, legs, and body organs.

The insect reproductive system is shown in detail on pages 108-117, and the skeletal and muscular systems are on the following pages.

Would you believe?

 A moth caterpillar weighing 0.1 oz. (2.8g) and 2.4 in. (6cm) long has about 1 1/2 million breathing tubes, each 0.24 in. (6mm) long, and 1 twenty-five-thousandth of an inch (1/1,000th mm) across at its smallest point. The total surface area of all the tubes is about 0.002 sq. in. (1.2 mm²).

INTERNAL BODY PARTS

Below are some of the main organs or body parts inside an insect's body.

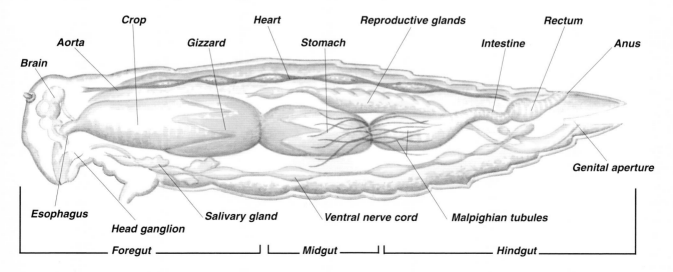

Brain • Aorta • Crop • Gizzard • Heart • Stomach • Reproductive glands • Intestine • Rectum • Anus

Genital aperture

Esophagus • Head ganglion • Salivary gland • Ventral nerve cord • Malpighian tubules

Foregut — Midgut — Hindgut

The Hard Case

The bug's body frame – the exoskeleton – is a tough, jointed casing worn on the outside.

The cuticle – here on a shiny scarab beetle – is the outermost portion of the exoskeleton. It has various layers, plus attachments such as hairs and bristles. The cuticle of the newly emerged beetle has a brilliant, metallic sheen, but this dulls as it is worn by the digging activites of its owner.

The shape, strength, and rigidity of an insect's body depends on its exoskeleton. This living suit of armor protects against injuries, predators, parasites, and disease. It is waterproof, and prevents the internal organs from drying or leaking their body fluids. It has tremendous strength, and provides both a framework for muscle anchorage, and a system of levers in the legs and wings for movement. Different parts of the exoskeleton are thick for strength, thin for flexibility, heavy for buoyancy in water, light for flight, and colored for warning or camouflage.

Three ingredients

The exoskeleton is made or secreted by glands in the skin. It has three chief components: chitin, sclerotin, and waxes. Chitin is a polysaccharide, tough yet flexible, and resistant to most chemicals. It is present throughout the body covering. Sclerotin, another protein, is strong and rigid. It is most concentrated in the hardest structures, like mouth parts, claws and spines, and nearly absent in joints. Waxes waterproof the insect, stopping moisture from getting in and body fluids from leaking out.

EXTERNAL AND INTERNAL SKELETONS

Humans and other mammals have an inner skeleton or endoskeleton, made of bones. So do birds, reptiles, amphibians, and fish.

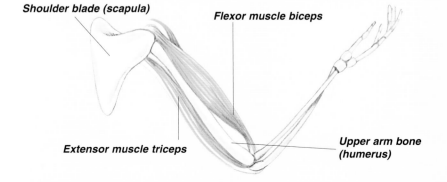

Shoulder blade (scapula)

Flexor muscle biceps

Extensor muscle triceps

Upper arm bone (humerus)

Skeletal plates

Structurally, the exoskeleton is made up of a series of plates known as sclerites, connected by flexible joints. The plates are named from their positions on one of the four body surfaces. These are the tergum or notum on the dorsal or upper surface, the pleura (singular pleuron) on each lateral or side surface, and the sternum on the ventral or lower surface. Tube-shaped sclerites form the legs, antennae, and similar appendages. The head is made of curved sclerites fused rigidly together.

Below

The cuticle is an essential feature of arthropod design. This illustration shows a section of typical insect cuticle.

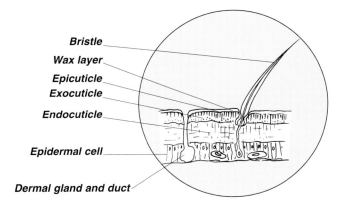

Bristle
Wax layer
Epicuticle
Exocuticle
Endocuticle
Epidermal cell
Dermal gland and duct

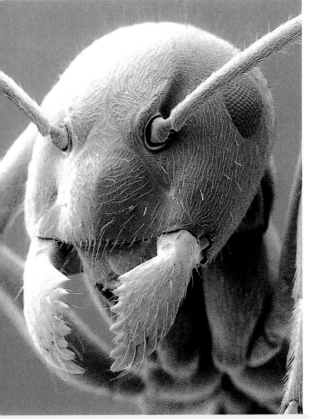

This electron microscope photograph of an ant's head shows how the insect cuticle is covered with sensory hairs and bristles.

Insects have an exoskeleton, like their other arthropod cousins, such as spiders and crabs. But both types of skeletons do similar jobs.

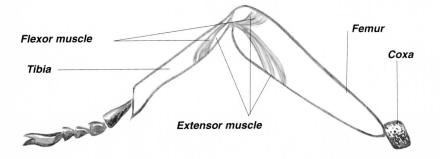

Flexor muscle

Tibia

Femur

Coxa

Extensor muscle

Would you believe?

Compared to the soft flesh of most animals, the insect exoskeleton is very resistant to rotting or decay. This was the main reason why entomology – the scientific study of insects – became so popular. Insect bodies could be collected and displayed in a lifelike state for centuries. The only precaution for preservation was to keep out more insects – living pests such as museum beetles.

Feats of Strength

Insects are incredibly strong for their size.
Rather, it is their small size that gives them great power.

There are several reasons why, for their size, insects are among the mightiest of all animals. Two are a result of the laws of biophysics (biology and physics). One says that as a body muscle becomes smaller, its total strength decreases – yet the relative force it can exert increases. Another shows that muscles on the inside of an exoskeleton can achieve greater leverage than muscles on the outside of an endoskeleton.

Pairs of muscles

The muscles are attached to sturdy internal projections of the exoskeleton called apodemes, either within an individual body segment, or across adjacent segments. Insect muscles are arranged like ours, in opposing or antagonistic pairs. As one muscle of a pair contracts, the other automatically relaxes to accommodate the motion. When the second muscle contracts, it produces movement in the opposite direction. In normal movements of the body, legs, and wings, many sets of paired muscles work together as teams.

Above

Male stag beetles use their huge "antlers" for fighting – with each other. They compete for the attention of the females. Their aim is to make their opponent helpless by using their bodily strength to flip him onto his back, where he is unable to move.

INSECT VERSUS HUMAN

• If a locust leg and a human leg were the same size, the locust's leg muscles would be 1,000 times more powerful!

• To beat the high-rise-building termites, humans would have to build an 800-storey skyscraper – without any machines or mechanical assistance!

• To match the strength of the stag beetle, a human would have to lift 10 tons with the mouth!

Direct delivery

In addition to their great strength, insect muscles do not tire very easily. This is due partly to the remarkable efficiency of the respiratory system. It delivers oxygen directly to the cells which make up the muscles, rather than delivering oxygen to the blood, which then carries it to the muscles, as in our own bodies. Compared to oxygen consumption at rest, during great activity the consumption increases a hundredfold. In the human body, it can only rise about thirtyfold.

Joined at joints

Insect joints are specialized thinned areas of the exoskeleton. Generally they work like hinges, moving to and fro in one plane only. So for a full range of motion, an appendage like a leg needs a series of joints oriented in different directions.

Would you believe?

• Termites, each less than ¼ in. (6mm) long, can build nests up to 10½ yds. (9.5m) tall – about 1500 times their own size. They can also dig wells 11¼ yds. (10m) deep.
• A stag beetle weighing ¼ oz. (7g) can pull a load of 1½ lbs. (680g), which is 97 times its own weight.
• Locusts can fly continuously, flapping their wings nonstop for nine hours.

Right

Some of the strongest muscles in the insect's body, in this case a termite, are within the chewing mouth parts. They clamp the insect's sharp mouth parts together to cut and crush the food.

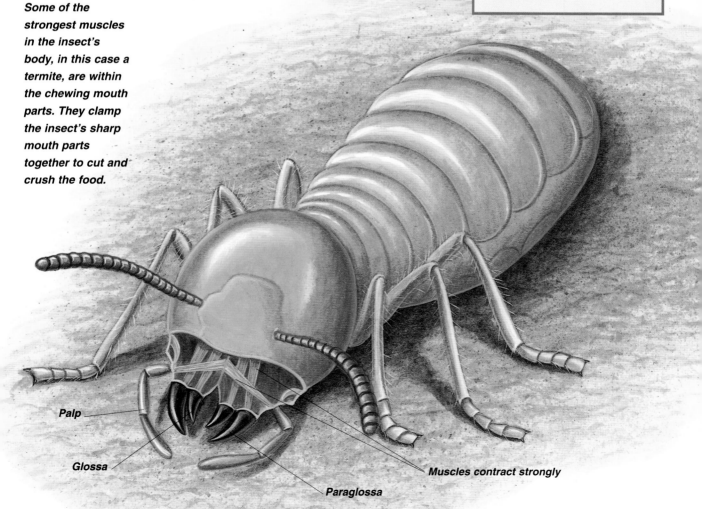

Palp

Glossa

Paraglossa

Muscles contract strongly

Wings to Fly

Insects were probably the first animals to take to the air and master flight.

The advantages of flight played a great role in the insects' success story. It allowed them to escape from ground-based predators, to become aerial predators themselves, and to cover long distances in search of suitable habitats, food, water, and mates. How did it all begin?

Gliding to flying

Insect wings probably originated as broad, flat extensions of the thorax exoskeleton. They allowed the bug to escape from enemies by gliding away after leaping from a branch or crag. In the process of evolution, over millions of years, occasional mutations produced insects with bigger and broader thoracic flanges. They glided better, survived, bred, and became more common. At some stage, they evolved muscles that could waggle their extensions. The rigid flaps evolved into flapping wings. For at least 100 million years, the early insects had the air to themselves.

Above

The cockchafer beetle crawls to a high vantage point before take-off. It opens and shuts its wing cases several times in pre-flight check, to warm up muscles and make sure everything is in order.

WINGS COMPARED

Four great groups of animals have evolved true flight, as opposed to gliding. These are the insects, pterosaurs (reptile contemporaries of the dinosaurs, all now extinct), birds, and bats. Insects are the only group of animals that developed appendages solely for flying. The wings of other flying animals evolved from limbs that were already present, used for walking, running, crawling, or climbing.

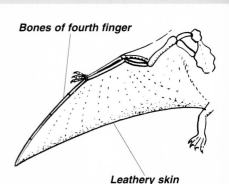

Pterosaur

Bones of fourth finger

Leathery skin

Fore and hind

Early flying insects had two pairs of wings that did not fold across each other or up over their body when at rest. Also, their forewings and hindwings flapped independently. Dragonflies and damselflies still display this design.

Further evolution led to the types of wings found in butterflies and bees. Each forewing and hindwing is linked by a hook and eye or similar mechanism, so they beat together. This forms two coordinated flight surfaces, left and right, instead of four.

Left

Like all flies, this cranefly has only one pair of wings, the forewings. The rear pair have evolved into "drumsticks" or halteres. These balancing organs function like spinning gyroscopes. They allow some flies to perform amazing aerobatics, such as hovering and flying backwards.

Balancers and wing covers

Flies have gone even one stage further. The first pair of wings are the flight surfaces. The hindwings have become tiny, ball-and-stick stabilizers called "halteres," which twirl around like mini-gyroscopes to steady the insect in flight.

Beetles evolved along another route. Their forewings have become wing cases, or elytra, which are hard covers over the back, designed to protect the delicate hindwings when these are folded out of the way. The elytra act as nonbeating aerofoils in the air; only the hindwings flap.

Would you believe?

The largest prehistoric dragonfly was *Meganeura monyi*, which lived 300 million years ago in France and had a wing span of 27½ in. (698mm).

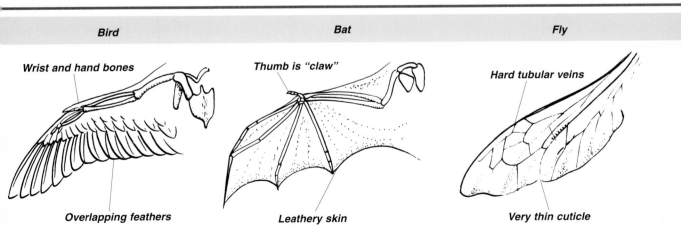

Bird

Wrist and hand bones

Overlapping feathers

Bat

Thumb is "claw"

Leathery skin

Fly

Hard tubular veins

Very thin cuticle

Wing Shape and Design

Wing shape and structure are major features in distinguishing and grouping insects.

Wings are so important for insect identification and classification that most insect orders (main groups) are named after their wing type. True flies, for example, belong to the order Diptera, which means "two wings." Butterflies and moths have membranous wings covered with minute, pigmented scales that create intricate, colorful patterns. Their order is Lepidoptera, which means "scale wings."

Sheathed and straight

The beetles and weevils, Coleoptera, are named from their "sheath wings." These bugs fold their large, membranous, delicate hindwings under the elytra – the forewings – which have evolved into hard wingcovers.

Grasshoppers and crickets have large, thin hindwings, and long, narrow, leathery forewings used for gliding. These are called tegmina. The name for this order, Orthoptera, translates as "straight wings."

The aptly named lacewing shows the delicate tracery of the wing veins. The pattern of veins is called venation. It is almost identical for all members of an insect species, and different from the venations of other species. This makes wings very useful when identifying and classifying bugs.

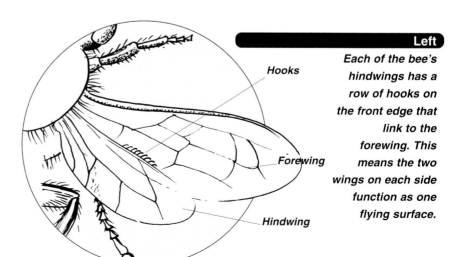

Hooks

Forewing

Hindwing

Left

Each of the bee's hindwings has a row of hooks on the front edge that link to the forewing. This means the two wings on each side function as one flying surface.

Left
This close-up of the wing of a Laurel swallowtail butterfly shows the tiny, colored scales that form the mosaic-like pattern.

Half and similar

The order name of the true bugs, Hemiptera, means "half wings." It refers to the forewings, which are thick and leathery along their fronts, with membranous tips. These wings fold over the more delicate hind-wings, which are the main flying ones.

Cicadas also have large, thin, delicately patterned wings. They belong to the Homoptera order, which means "similar wings." Some experts rank the Homoptera as a suborder of the main order Hemiptera. Others consider that homopterans should have the status of an order. There are many such discussions and disagreements when studying bugs!

Would you believe?

Insect wings get their shape and strength from their frame-work of darker, thicker, tube-like parts called veins. However, in most insects, these veins do not carry blood, except when they first unfold and expand as the adult insect emerges from its last molt and "pumps up" its wings. The veins soon dry out and remain in the wings as stiffening rods.

• The largest wing spans of living insects belong to the Atlas moth (*Attacus*) of India and the great owlet moth (*Thysania zenobia*) of South America. Both may exceed 12 in. (30cm).

• The largest dragonfly in the world today, *Megaloprepus caeruleata*, has a wing span of 7½ in. (191mm); it lives in Central America.

Taking Flight

Insect wings work on the energy-efficient "clickbox" principle.

Dragonflies are exceptionally skilled fliers. They can hover in mid air, go straight up, and even fly backwards for short distances.

Insect wings are moved mainly by two groups of indirect flight muscles housed in the middle-body part, the thorax. The muscles are called indirect because they are not attached to the wings themselves. They pull on the thorax's exoskeleton plates, or sclerites, to "click" them from a convex shape to a concave one. The same principle is used in clickbox toys and gadgets. It is very energy efficient, since energy is stored in the plates after each click.

Pivotal point

The wings are wedged between the flexing exoskeletal plates. As the plates flick from concave to convex and back again, the wings move by leverage, about a pivotal point called the fulcrum. Smaller direct flight muscles adjust the angle of the upstroke and downstroke for forward propulsion and steering.

Beats and speeds

The wingbeat frequency in beats per minute, and the speed of flying, vary greatly from species to species. Insects with light bodies and large wings, like butterflies, need a relatively slow wingbeat frequency. Bugs with smaller wings and relatively heavy bodies, such as flies and bees, flap much faster. Also, smaller bugs tend to beat their wings faster than larger ones.

HOW FAST DO THEY FLAP?

Wingbeat rate comparisons
(one beat equals the upstroke plus the downstroke):
• The tiny midge *Forcipomyia* flaps its wings 62,760 times each minute. This means its flight muscles contract and relax in a cycle lasting 0.0009 seconds – the quickest in the animal kingdom.
• A housefly flaps its wings at 18,000 beats per minute.
• A bee's wingbeat rate is 12,000 per minute.
• The slowest insect wingbeat is that of the swallowtail butterfly, at 300 beats per minute.

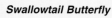

Swallowtail Butterfly

Bee

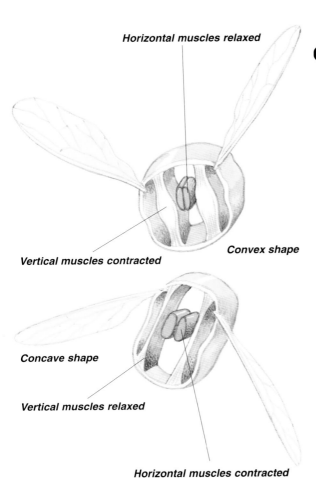

Horizontal muscles relaxed

Vertical muscles contracted

Convex shape

Concave shape

Vertical muscles relaxed

Horizontal muscles contracted

The rigid thorax of a flying insect functions like a clickbox mechanism. As the horizontal flight muscles pull on the sides of the thorax, they flip or click from a convex to a concave shape, like the sides of a tin can, and tilt the wings down. When the vertical flight muscles contract, the thorax compresses, and the sides then click back, which pivots the wings up.

Would you believe?

• Bees fly at 5-9 miles (8-15km) per hour.
• Some botflies, hawkmoths, tropical butterflies, and horseflies fly at up to 25-35 miles (40-55km) per hour.
• Some Australian dragonflies have a top speed of 35-40 miles (55-65km) per hour.
• In 1926, an American zoologist claimed he saw a deer botfly whiz past him at 800 mph. (1,300km/h). Even though he had no measuring equipment, the record stood for many years, but is now discredited.

Warming up

Insect bodies work best when they are warm. The body temperature is regulated primarily by the temperature of the surroundings. On a chilly day, an insect may rapidly vibrate its wings to get its flight muscles working and generating heat, ready for take-off. It may also bask in a patch of sunshine with wings outspread; here, the wings act as solar panels to absorb heat.

The bumblebee's body is very heavy, and near the upper limit for the kind of flapping flight that insects use.

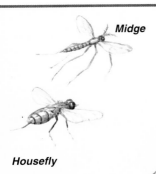

Midge

Housefly

End of upstroke

End of downstroke

Legs and Lifestyle

The legs of an insect indicate its lifestyle – digger, leaper, waterwalker, fast runner, or slow crawler.

Adult insects usually have six legs, and each leg consists of five sections. The first is the coxa, joined to the thorax by a ball and socket joint. The next section, the femur, is the largest, and is packed with muscles. Next is the tibia, which often has spines or a pair of movable spurs to improve grip. Fourth is the tarsus, or foot, which itself consists of five smaller sections. It is tipped by the fifth section, a pair of strong claws, and often has sticky pads or glands.

A multitude of adaptations

Many insects use their legs for walking and crawling, and as springy landing gear to cushion their touchdown after flying. But legs can have many other functions, and in some insects, the three pairs are shaped very differently.

Above

The water boatman swims upside-down, rowing with its third pair of legs. They are long and fringed with tough hairs, so they work like oars.

Insects that live underground, like mole crickets and dung beetles, have broad, shovel-shaped legs, sometimes armed with heavy spines for digging. Predators like mantids, giant water bugs, and ambush bugs have raptorial forelegs. These are long and strong, and are adapted for seizing, holding, and killing prey.

Hanging baskets

Dragonfly and damselfly legs are long and slender, with rows of stiff bristles. In flight, they hang down like a loose basket to scoop prey from the air. This is how these predators catch their victims.

Bugs that crawl, run, leap, and swim are shown on the following pages.

Larval legs

The young forms or larvae of most insects walk on the usual six thoracic legs. But they are not always as adept at getting around as their parents. The caterpillars – larvae of butterflies and moths – also have abdominal prolegs that move in waves. The hind pair are carried forward first and the others follow in succession.

Geometrid moth caterpillars move by arching their body to bring their prolegs forward, then straightening to reach ahead with their thoracic legs. This looping motion has led to their nickname of "inchworms."

Would you believe?

• When the female vaporer moth emerges from her pupal stage to mate with a waiting male, she lays her eggs on the remains of her pupal case and dies – without having ever moved!
• Lice have prehensile claws on the ends of their legs that allow them to hang on effortlessly to the hairs of their hosts. The claws are shaped differently, according to a cross section of the type of hair to which they cling.
• Sloth moths cling to the hairs of tree-hanging sloths, only letting go of their tight hold during the animal's once-weekly toilet trip. The moths then lay their eggs in the sloth's feces.

Notch

Comb

Basket

Left

Each pair of a honeybee's legs has a different job. The front or first pair have special notches so the bee can clean its head, antennae, and eyes. The middle or second pair have combs to sweep pollen from body hairs into the bristly pollen baskets. The baskets are on the rear or third pair

Walkers and Runners

All winged insects can fly, yet many rely on walking or running as their main method of moving.

Many insect legs are designed simply for walking, like wasps, or for running, like tiger beetles and cockroaches. In the standard method of walking, the body is always supported by a tripod formed by the front and hind legs on one side and the middle leg on the other side.

To make a stride, a trio of legs is lifted in the consecutive order of front, middle, and hind leg, each swung forward and put down. Then the other three legs go through the same process. The effect is that all three feet on each side touch down in succession on the same spot of ground. The hind legs provide most of the propulsion and turning force.

Like the water strider, the pond skater walks easily on the water's surface, using the surface tension film to stay afloat on its long middle, and back legs.

On the ceiling

Many insects can walk where other animals cannot, such as on ceilings or other upside-down surfaces, on vertical walls, and even on smooth windows. A wall or ceiling may seem perfectly smooth to us, but at the small-sized scale of insects, it has minute imperfections, rough enough to be gripped with the insect's sharp, tarsal claws. Some insects also have sticky, cushion-like adhesive organs called pulvilli (see opposite).

LEGS FOR DIFFERENT JOBS

The saucer bug and praying mantis use their viciously armed front legs to help them trap and kill their victims. Mole crickets and scarab beetles have shovel-shaped legs for digging. Crickets have powerful hind legs for running and jumping. The tiger beetle is a land-speed record holder, using its long legs to sprint. The suction pads and bristles on a male great diving beetle's front legs help him to grasp a female during mating.

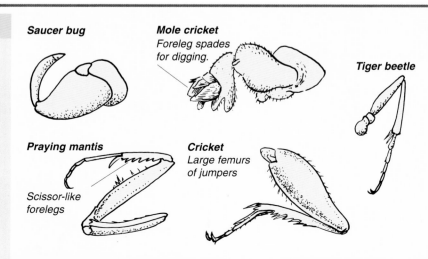

Saucer bug

Mole cricket
Foreleg spades for digging.

Tiger beetle

Praying mantis
Scissor-like forelegs

Cricket
Large femurs of jumpers

Left

The ends of an insect's legs usually have a pair of claws. But the fly's foot also has hairs and a wide, sticky, suction pad that can cling even to glossy leaves.

Would you believe?

• The record-breaking running insect is a tropical cockroach that can race along at 3½ miles (5.6km) per hour.
• In Texas and Mexico, water striders are sometimes called "Jesus bugs," because of their ability to walk on water.

One family of bugs, the water striders (Gerridae), can walk on water without sinking in – and without getting their feet wet! Their spindly middle and hind legs distribute their light bodyweight over a large area, so it does not break the "skin" or surface film on the water. Also, the legs and body have tiny hairs which form a velvety, water-repellent covering. On the feet, the tarsal claws are located well back from the tip, so they do not pierce the water's surface tension.

Below left

The sticky, sponge-like pads called pulvilli on a fly's feet can grip glass, plastic, metal or gloss paint.

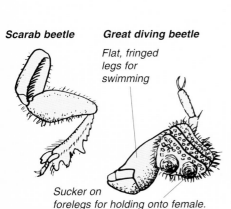

Scarab beetle

Great diving beetle

Flat, fringed legs for swimming

Sucker on forelegs for holding onto female.

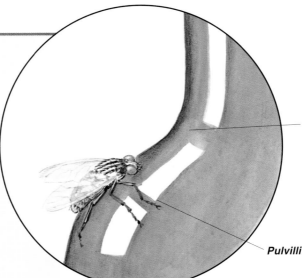

Glass bottle

Pulvilli

Jumpers and Leapers

Jumping insects rely on very muscular hind legs to launch themselves into the air – usually to escape.

Jumping insects include grasshoppers, crickets, locusts, leafhoppers, fleas, flea beetles, springtails, and click beetles. They have relatively long hindlegs with greatly enlarged femurs. The main power for the jump comes from incredibly strong muscles in the femur and the other long-leg section, the tibia. At rest, these two sections are folded at a sharp angle.

Legs and wings

When a grasshopper prepares to jump, it brings each tibia even closer into the body, near its center of gravity, and then suddenly contracts the large muscles within to straighten the leg. This hurls the insect in a forward arc. It may land nearby, open its wings to glide further, or even flap them to fly away.

Above

A flea executes its amazing high jumps by storing energy in its thorax. The thorax muscles bend into a dome shape until the flea wants to jump. Then the muscles relax, and the thorax springs into its flatter shape, which pulls the insect's legs straight and sends it high into the air.

Gaps between leaps

Most leaping insects, including grasshoppers, must rest momentarily between jumps. Their muscles are relatively few and simple in structure and design, and they need a short time to recover. This contrasts with the more complex and numerous muscles and joints of mammals and birds, who can run and leap in a continuous manner.

Jump in the air

Click beetles or skipjacks do not leap away from danger. They play dead and fall off their perch. But if they land upside-down on their backs, or on their hard wingcovers (elytra), they can only right themselves by flicking up into the air. Their muscles suddenly pull a backward-pointing spine on the underside of the thorax into a cavity, which makes the wingcovers flip open. These push against the ground and jerk the beetle into the air.

Would you believe?

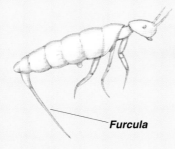

• Springtails *(Collembola)* are very ancient, flightless insects that leap using a different mechanism from other insect groups. The forked, spring-like "tail," the furcula, is normally held under the body by a clip. To jump, the springtail releases the clip and the tail flicks backwards, hurling the insect into the air!

Furcula

• Some jumping insects experience "g" forces (the force due to gravity) of 100g. The human limit is about 5g.

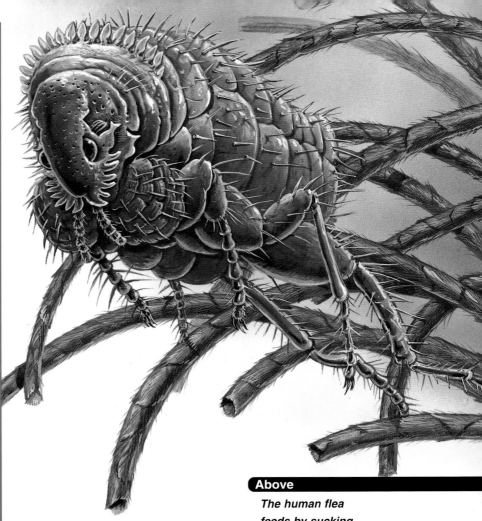

Above

The human flea feeds by sucking blood, holding onto nearby hairs as it does so. It uses its amazing jumping power to transfer to a new host in between meals.

HIGH JUMP AND LONG JUMP: INSECTS VERSUS HUMANS

• The world's largest grasshopper is 10 in. (25cm) long. It can long jump 5¼ yds. (4.8m). This is equivalent to a human long jumping over 98 ft. (30m). The human record is about 29½ ft. (8.95m).
• The common flea can high jump almost 8 in. (20cm), about 130 times its own height. This would be like a human high jumping 722 ft. (220m) over a 60-storey skyscraper. The human world record is about 8 ft. (2.5m).
• The flea can also jump 12¾ in. (32cm) horizontally, which is equivalent to a human long jump of 394 ft. (120m).

Living in Water

Insects evolved on land, breathing air. Yet many have taken to water for part or all of their lives.

Aquatic or water-dwelling insects have two obstacles to overcome. One is getting oxygen; the other is moving around.

Oxygen can be obtained from air, or dissolved in water. Strong swimmers have no trouble getting to the surface for a breath of fresh air. Many water beetles pick up a bubble of air and carry it back down. Water scorpions and the aquatic larvae (young) of many insects breathe through a snorkel-like tube that pierces the surface film.

Above

A great diving beetle has its own air – the shiny bubble on its rear end.

Breathing underwater

The nymphs or naiads (young) of many insects – mayflies, stoneflies, caddisflies, and dragonflies – do not come to the surface for air. They breathe like fish, using gills. The feathery tracheal gills take in oxygen, which is dissolved in the water.

Sand

Small pebbles

Twigs

BUILDING HOMES

Caddisfly larvae (Trichoptera) build houses out of sand, twigs, or whatever is available to protect their soft bodies. The larva carries its dwelling everywhere for protection, and also to counteract its natural buoyancy and keep it on the bottom. Different species use different materials:

- *Glyphtotaelius pellucidus* builds with flat beech leaves.
- *Phryganea* uses pieces of rolled leaf.
- *Limnephilus vittatus* builds with sand grains.
- *Sericostoma* also favors sand grains.
- *Silo* constructs with sand and small pebbles.
- *Anabolia* uses sand grains and twigs.

Caddisfly larvae

Fast flow

Aquatic insects are adapted to the water currents of their habitat. Inhabitants of swift streams and rivers, like stonefly larvae, usually present a low profile. They have flattened bodies to avoid the current, and wide-set, strongly gripping legs to hang onto the bottom.

Swimmers

Active swimmers, such as giant water bugs, backswimmers, water boatmen, diving beetles, and water scavenger beetles, have long, oar-like hind legs. Rows of close-set hairs fold in on the forward stroke and then flare open on the back stroke, which provides extra push. These swimmers are often boat-shaped, with a keel-like body, and a smooth, slippery cuticle.

   In still ponds and lakes, many insects are nonswimmers. They get around by creeping and crawling among the vegetation.

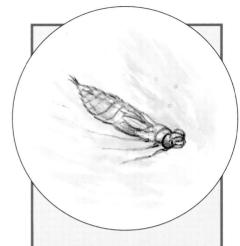

Would you believe?

 Dragonfly nymphs are jet propelled! The respiratory system normally works by slowly drawing water into the abdomen through the anal opening and passing it over rectal gills to absorb dissolved oxygen. But the nymph can contract its abdominal muscles and eject this water with explosive force, jetting itself forward to pursue prey or elude enemies.

Left

Water scorpions are not good swimmers. Their legs are better at walking along the bottom. The front pair form two jackknives that grab passing small fish or tadpoles.

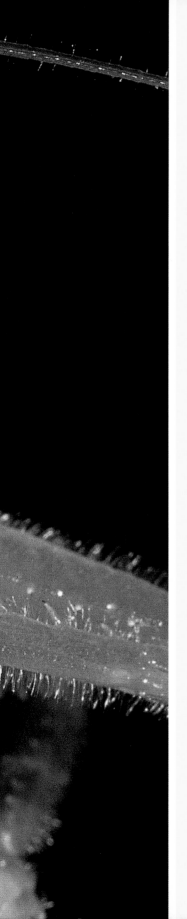

2

SENSES AND COMMUNICATION

BUGS HAVE VERY HIGHLY ADVANCED AND UNUSUAL SENSES, WHICH THEY RELY ON FOR VARIOUS PURPOSES — FOR FINDING FOOD, DETECTING PREDATORS, AND FOR COMMUNICATING WITH EACH OTHER. THEY HAVE A UNIQUE BLEND OF TOUCH, TASTE, AND SMELL SENSES, WHICH ARE JOINED TOGETHER IN CHEMORECEPTORS ALL OVER THEIR BODIES, ENABLING, FOR EXAMPLE, THE GRASSHOPPER SHOWN HERE TO "TASTE" THE FLOWER'S SCENT WITH ITS LEGS.

MOST INSECTS HAVE TWO DIFFERENT TYPES OF EYES, BUT ALTHOUGH WE KNOW MUCH ABOUT THESE, WE CAN ONLY GUESS AT WHAT THE BUG ACTUALLY "SEES." MANY INSECTS ARE NOT ONLY ABLE TO SEE IN THE DARK, BUT CAN ALSO GLOW IN THE DARK THROUGH A SPECIAL CHEMICAL CAPACITY FOR EMITTING LIGHT FLASHES.

BUGS USUALLY HEAR BY SENSING SOUND THROUGH THEIR SKIN, AND ALTHOUGH THEY DON'T HAVE "VOICES," THEY CAN PRODUCE AN AMAZING VARIETY OF SOUNDS TO WARD OFF ENEMIES, ATTRACT MATES, AND COMMUNICATE TO OTHERS IN THEIR COLONIES.

FOR MOST BUGS, THOUGH, THE WORLD IS DOMINATED BY SMELLS AND TASTES, AND FOR THIS THEY HAVE DEVELOPED "FEELERS" OR ANTENNAE TO HELP THEM FURTHER PERCEIVE THEIR ENVIRONMENT.

Senses and Communication

Insects use their highly tuned senses to survive and to communicate with each other – and with other animals.

Many flowers have violet or purple petals that attract bees and similar insects

We experience the world through sights, sounds, smells, tastes, and touches. Insects have similar main senses, but they work in different ways. Most adult insects have well-developed eyes, that help them to see prey or other food, and to detect predators and other dangers. Like us, they see in color, and they have two eyes to judge distance (stereoscopic vision). In certain ways, their vision is better than ours. Some insects can see all around themselves, by day and at night. They are sensitive to infrared light, ultraviolet light, and polarized light, which we are not.

Chemical senses

Despite excellent vision, the world for many bugs is dominated by scents and tastes. These are in the form of natural chemical substances. Smell and taste often blur together, and are detected in combined form by chemoreceptors all over the bug's body. Insects use their chemosenses to test their surroundings and to find food and mates. Many insects are also sensitive, as we are, to gravity, temperature, and humidity, and also to magnetism, which we aren't.

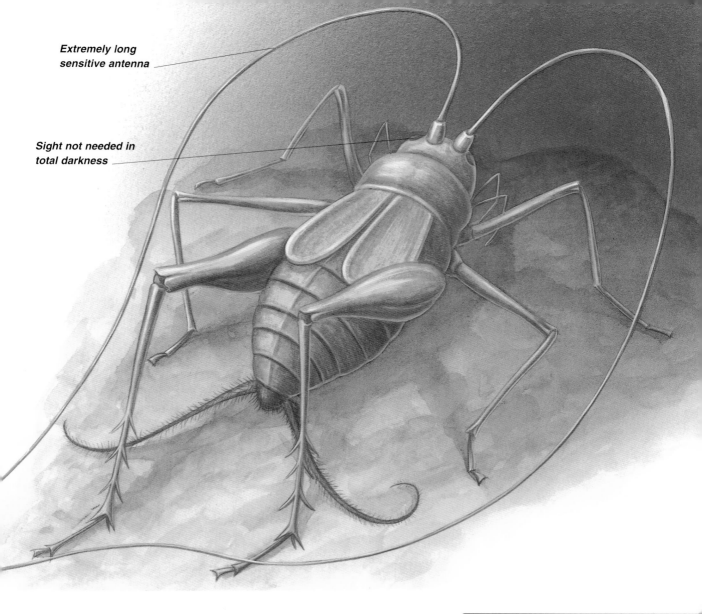

Extremely long
sensitive antenna

Sight not needed in
total darkness

Talking to others

Most insects communicate with others of their kind only at mating time.
They use a fascinating array of colors and patterns, songs and dances,
light shows, scents, and physical contests to beat rivals and to attract
partners. When they communicate with other creatures, it's usually to
catch a victim for a meal – or to avoid becoming one. Their attack-and-
defense arsenal includes warning colors and noises, camouflage and
disguise, chemical warfare, and other shock tactics.

Social insects – chiefly bees, wasps, ants, and termites – have very
sophisticated communication to keep order in the colony. They use
sights, sounds, touches, and also pheromones. These scent-like
chemicals spread among their members in the air and by contact.

Above

*In total darkness,
sight is useless. So
cave crickets are
blind, but their other
senses help to
compensate.
The cricket's
extraordinary, long
antennae can feel,
smell, and even hear
what's going on
around them.*

Through Insect Eyes

We know the detailed structure and workings of insect eyes – but we can only guess what the bug "sees" in its brain.

Most adult insects have two types of eyes. Simple eyes are called ocelli. Each has one tiny, light-receiving area. A single ocellus can only detect levels of light, from dark to bright. It cannot form a picture or image. There are usually several ocelli on the front and top of the head. Most young insects have only ocelli, or simple eyes.

Eye of many parts

The other type of insect eye is the compound eye. It is usually rounded and bulging – the typical "bug eye." Its surface has many separate parts called facets. Each is the light-focusing lens of a cone-shaped, light-sensing unit beneath, called an ommatidium.

Since the compound eye is bulging, the ommatidia point in all different directions, so the insect can see most of its surroundings without moving its head. The overall image is probably made up of many small areas or mosaic-like patches, one for each ommatidium. But how the bug brain interprets and experiences the scene is still a mystery.

Above

A dragonfly often "buzzes" an intruder in its territory to get a closer look. Thousands of tiny facets in each eye give a very detailed view of the scene, like the tiny dots that make up a printed picture.

COLOR VISION

Insect eyes can see a wider part of the light spectrum than our own eyes, especially towards the violet and ultraviolet end. The visible spectrum is made up of different colors or wavelengths of light (a nanometer or nm is one-millionth of a millimeter).

Ultraviolet 5 to 400 nm
Violets 400 to 450 nm
Blues 450 to 500 nm
Greens 500 to 575 nm
Yellows 575 to 625 nm
Oranges 625 to 700 nm
Reds 700 to 800 nm
Infrared 800 to 1,000,000 nm

Human eye 397 to 770 nm
Insect range varies between 10 and 900 nm
Butterfly eye 10 to 650 nm
Honeybee 300 to 700 nm

Short sight

Most insects are naturally short-sighted. Farther things look more blurred. However, insect eyes are excellent at detecting motion. As an object such as a fly goes past, its image flicks across adjacent ommatidia, giving precise information about speed and direction.

Seeing in the dark

The insect eye can adjust to a wide range of light levels using the iris cells. These contain grains of a pigment or coloring substance. The grains spread out in bright light, forming a shaded screen that works like sunglasses to reduce glare. Night-active insects usually have some combination of larger eyes, bigger facets, longer ommatidia, and fewer iris cells to let in more light.

Some insects can also detect the direction of polarized light, which means they can tell the position of the sun even on a cloudy day. This is a valuable aid to finding their way, especially when migrating.

Would you believe?

These are the numbers of facets per compound eye:

• Cave-dwelling crickets, some beetles, springtails, and bristletails have none. They lack compound eyes.

• In some species of ants, the worker has 6 facets in each eye; the queen or fertile female has 200; and the male who pursues her has 400.

• Male glowworms (see page 51) have 2,500 facets, while females have 300.

• Houseflies have 4,000.

• Diving beetles have 9,000.

• Butterflies have up to 17,000 facets.

• Dragonflies, who are swift aerial hunters, have up to 50,000.

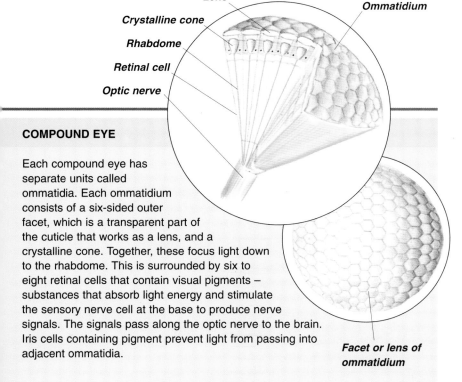

Lens

Crystalline cone

Rhabdome

Retinal cell

Optic nerve

Ommatidium

Facet or lens of ommatidium

COMPOUND EYE

Each compound eye has separate units called ommatidia. Each ommatidium consists of a six-sided outer facet, which is a transparent part of the cuticle that works as a lens, and a crystalline cone. Together, these focus light down to the rhabdome. This is surrounded by six to eight retinal cells that contain visual pigments – substances that absorb light energy and stimulate the sensory nerve cell at the base to produce nerve signals. The signals pass along the optic nerve to the brain. Iris cells containing pigment prevent light from passing into adjacent ommatidia.

Fantastic Light Displays

Some insects send visual signals by flashing lights – produced by their own bodies.

The young or larva of the fungus gnat dangles silk threads spotted with glue, and then lies in its tube, glowing. The glue beads light up and attract moths.

Hundreds of types of insect glow in the dark! The best-known light makers are the fireflies and glow-worms. These are neither flies or worms, but are both types of beetle. With fireflies, it's mainly the males that shine, while with glowworms, it's the females. Other types of beetle also make light, along with some midges, fungus gnats, and springtails.

Colored and flashing lights

The color of insect light varies with the species – it's usually yellow or green. But one type of tropical glowworm emits red light from its head and a green glow from its sides. And the tropical cucujos, a kind of click beetle (*Pyrophorus*), makes a red light in flight that changes to green on landing.

Only fireflies can flash – turn their lights on and off rapidly. They control the light-generating or photogenic organs by nerves from the brain. Not all species of fireflies produce light. Those that do are active and glow at night all through their life cycle – even from the eggs!

The mating signal

Why do insects glow or flash at all? It is usually to locate and identify mates at breeding time. Each species produces its own light color and signal patterns, usually at a certain time during the night. This helps to avoid confusion during the breeding season, when many insects are active and searching for partners.

Female fireflies recognize the flashing pattern of males as they fly by. They respond with their own flashes, from their perch on low vegetation. The male zooms in, lands, and mates. The female then lays luminous eggs in the soil, which hatch into glowing larvae.

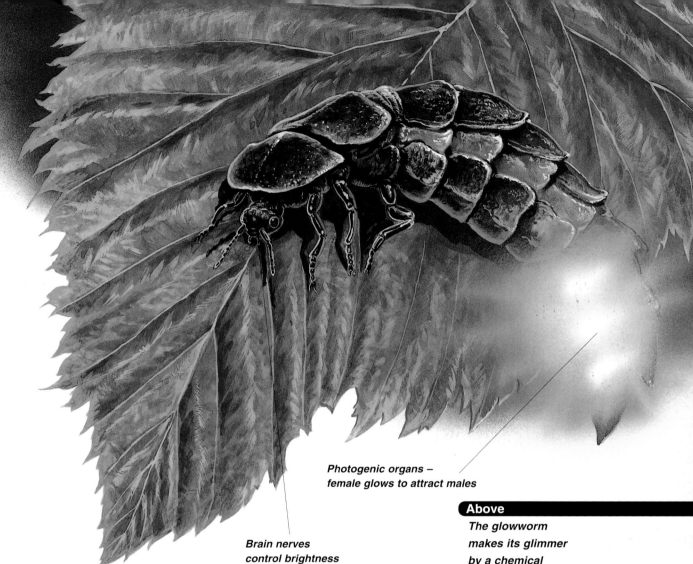

Photogenic organs –
female glows to attract males

Brain nerves
control brightness

Above

*The glowworm
makes its glimmer
by a chemical
reaction. This
takes place in
photogenic organs
at the end of the
abdomen, near the
tail tip. Nerves
from the brain
control the light's
brightness.*

LET THERE BE LIGHT!

• Insects make light by chemical means. A pigment chemical called luciferin combines with oxygen, helped by the enzyme luciferase.

• This chemical change happens continuously in special photogenic or light-producing organs.

• Unlike the light from our bulbs and candles, insect light has almost no heat released with it.

• Compared to the light and heat from a candle flame, an insect making light of similar brightness would produce only 1/80,000th as much heat.

Would you believe?

• The predatory female firefly *Photuris* flashes to a male of her own species, attracts him, and mates. Then she mimics the flashing signals of female *Photinus* fireflies. When a male of this kind lands nearby, expecting to find a mate, she eats him – a victim of fatal attraction!

Active at night

Most insects that glow in the dark are nocturnal – active only at night – or they live in dark places, such as caves. Fireflies and glowworms only flash in the dark, so that their displays are seen to best effect. Indeed, light production is of little use during daylight hours!

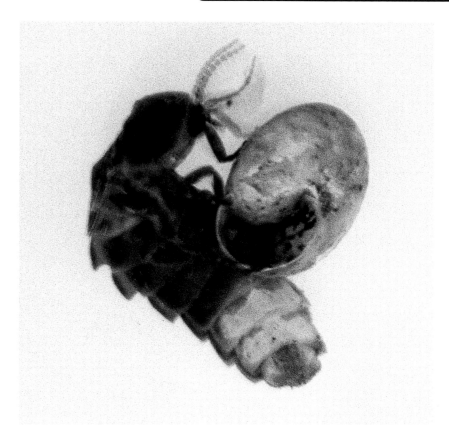

This Mexican firefly (Quintana roo) sits on the edge of a leaf at dusk, flashing its abdomen as a signal and scanning the landscape with its huge, beady eyes, in search of a response.

Do you know...

• *Question:* How many glowworms does it take to **equal** a light-bulb?
Answer: The electrical light power of 8,000 glowworms is roughly equivalent to an 100-watt lightbulb!

  Glowworms produce about one-fortieth of a candle's light power. However, they are 90 percent efficient (only 10 percent of their energy turns to heat), whereas an ordinary lightbulb is only 3 percent efficient.

Female glowworms produce light almost all through their lives, from egg to adult. This larva is gorging itself on one of its favorite foods, a small snail. It pours digestive juices from its mouth into the snail's shell, to dissolve the victim's flesh. Then it drinks the soupy results. Yet it continues to shine during its meal. As night falls the glow changes from greenish-yellow to bright yellow.

Listening In

Some insects have good hearing, but for most, it's not their sharpest sense.

On a warm summer's afternoon, meadows buzz and chirrup with the songs of male grasshoppers. The females listen to the serenade and move around so that the "ears on their knees" can pinpoint the exact position of the most attractive-sounding male.

Most insects detect sound waves by feeling, rather than by hearing as we do with our ears. The insect's outer "skin" or cuticle has tiny hair sensillae, each with a nerve-rich ball-and-socket base. This detects movement of the hair caused by sound waves in the air or by touch. Hair sensillae are found on the antennae, scattered randomly over the body, and in cockroaches and crickets, clustered around the rear end on flaps called anal cerci.

Insect ears

Several types of insect have more ear-like tympanic organs, similar to our eardrums, one on each side of the body. They consist of a thin, but tough and flexible membrane, stretched across a rigid, hollow structure. The membrane vibrates when struck by sound waves. These vibrations pass along cord-like chordotonal sensillae and generate nerve signals that go to the brain.

Hearing mates

Insects with tympanic membranes include crickets, grasshoppers, and cicadas. In crickets and long-horned grasshoppers, they are positioned on the front of the tibia of each foreleg. Cicadas have them on the lower abdominal surface, near the thorax. Hearing is important because these bugs make and listen to sounds at breeding time, to find mates. Other insects have tympanic organs on the sides of the thorax or the first abdominal segment.

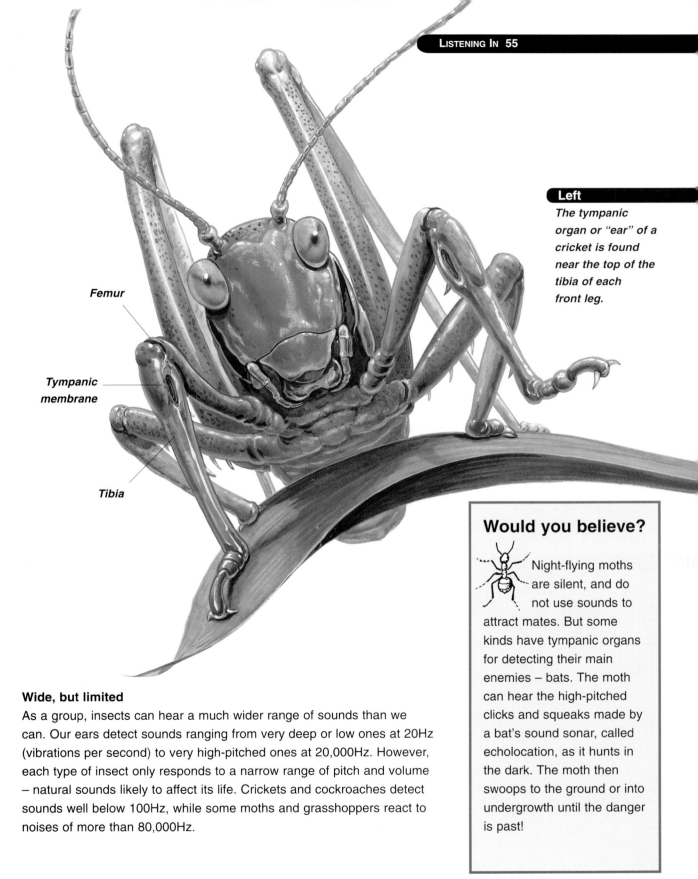

Femur

Tympanic
membrane

Tibia

Left
The tympanic organ or "ear" of a cricket is found near the top of the tibia of each front leg.

Would you believe?

Night-flying moths are silent, and do not use sounds to attract mates. But some kinds have tympanic organs for detecting their main enemies – bats. The moth can hear the high-pitched clicks and squeaks made by a bat's sound sonar, called echolocation, as it hunts in the dark. The moth then swoops to the ground or into undergrowth until the danger is past!

Wide, but limited

As a group, insects can hear a much wider range of sounds than we can. Our ears detect sounds ranging from very deep or low ones at 20Hz (vibrations per second) to very high-pitched ones at 20,000Hz. However, each type of insect only responds to a narrow range of pitch and volume – natural sounds likely to affect its life. Crickets and cockroaches detect sounds well below 100Hz, while some moths and grasshoppers react to noises of more than 80,000Hz.

Sound Systems

Insects make sounds to warn off enemies, attract mates, and pass information to their colony members.

Insects do not have "voices" that come from their mouths, as we do. But they can make many characteristic sounds by tapping, rubbing, scraping, or vibrating some part of their body, such as a wing or leg, or by blowing air from their breathing tubes out through the spiracles.

Scratches and scrapes

Rubbing or scraping one body part against another is called stridulation. This is the way that grasshoppers, katydids, crickets, water boatmen, and dung beetles make sounds. Usually, only the male stridulates to attract a female at mating time.

These types of insects usually "sing" during regular periods of activity. Day-active grasshoppers and cicadas stridulate mainly during daylight hours and towards dusk. Most male katydids serenade their females at night. Crickets, however, chirp and chirrup both by day and night.

MAKING LOVE SONGS

Insects stridulate by rubbing, scraping, or scratching one body part against another. They do it in various ways.
• Short-horned grasshoppers and locusts have a row of about 80 fine spines on the femur of each back leg. They rub these to and fro against a projecting vein on the outside of each leathery forewing, or tegmena. (Rub your fingernail along a comb for the same effect.)
• Long-horned grasshoppers and crickets have a hardened scraper on one forewing and a prominent, file-like vein on the other, which they rub together.
• Water boatmen scratch a patch of pegs on the front femur against a sharp edge on the head.
• Dung beetles scrape a ridged area of the hind leg against the base of the second leg.

Squeaks and screams

June beetles, lubber grasshoppers, queen honeybees, sphinx moth caterpillars, and some flies can make squeaking noises when disturbed. They squeeze the abdomen and force air out of the narrowed breathing holes, the spiracles.

The death's-head sphinx moth even screams like us. It makes a high-pitched sound by forcing air out of its mouth. Male Australian whistling moths produce their courtship song by moving hollow, bowl-shaped structures on their wings.

Clicks and taps

Ants can produce clicks by clacking their mandibles ("jaws") together, or even by hitting a solid object like a piece of wood with their heads. The rate and volume of clicks sends messages to others in the nest.

Some butterflies and moths, among them the calico butterflies of the tropical Americas, click their wings together in flight.

Stag-beetle larvae and deathwatch beetles tap as they burrow through decaying wood. In fact, the deathwatch got its name by tapping on old oak beams in houses to attract a mate. The eerie noise worried the people living there, who thought it was the souls of the dead!

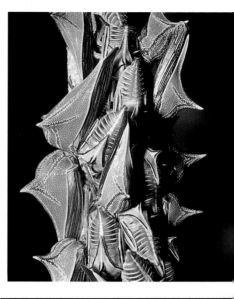

Above

Recently, experts discovered that leafhoppers, thornbugs and planthoppers have similar sound-producing organs to their cicada cousins.

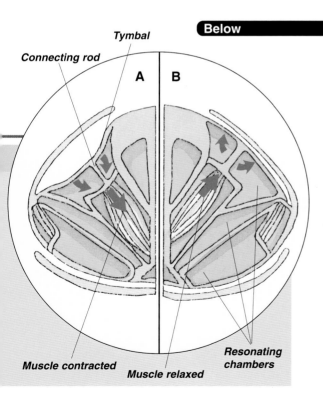

Below

Cicadas chirp using a pair of drum-like organs on each side of the first abdominal segment. (A) A thin membrane, called the tymbal, is pulled inwards by a connecting rod joined to a large muscle. (B) When the muscle relaxes, the membrane clicks back to its original shape. The clicks are made louder or amplified by hollow, resonating chambers.

Tymbal

Connecting rod

A | B

Muscle contracted

Muscle relaxed

Resonating chambers

Would you believe?

Snowy tree crickets (*Oecanthus fultoni*) make one of the most common summer-night sounds in North America. Males sing to attract mates – and also act as a thermometer. Like other muscle-powered insect actions, stridulation gets faster as the insect gets warmer.

Touch and Balance

Most bugs are covered with tiny receptors that sense contact, temperature, and other aspects of touch.

Above

Like all insects, this Saturn moth's body and legs are covered with stiff hairs or bristles. These have sensitive nerves at their bases (similar to our own body hairs), which send nerve signals to the brain whenever the hair is moved.

The basic design for an insect's touch or tactile receptor is a small hair or larger bristle called a seta (sensilla), with a ball-and-socket joint at its base, embedded in the cuticle. The seta itself is hard and unfeeling, but the joint has a network of microscopic nerve fibers that detect movement. This design is adapted to sense not only physical contact, but also air, wind, and water currents, and even the pull of gravity.

Which way is up?

Georeceptors or statocysts are the versions that detect gravity. They also provide the bug with information about its balance, orientation, and speed and direction of movement. A statocyst is a fluid-filled chamber lined with setae and containing a solid granule called a statolith. As the insect moves about, the statolith rolls around the chamber, and the setae detect its position and path.

Statocysts are useful for walking, burrowing, swimming, and flying. Aquatic insects also have tiny air bubbles within their tracheal or breathing tubes. The tubes have sensitive linings, and detect the position of the bubbles as they move to the highest part of the tube, much like a builder's spirit level.

Knowing where your legs are

Insects, like us, also have proprioceptors or stretch receptors. They are microscopic, specialized cells within joints and muscles that send out nerve signals according to how much they are stressed or stretched. This provides information about the positions and angles of the bug's legs, antennae, and other body parts.

Changes in the weather

Some insect microsensors are less understood. Thermoreceptors monitor temperature, allowing the bug to avoid unsuitable conditions of heat or cold. Baroreceptors detect pressure changes. This helps terrestrial insects to sense atmospheric pressure and to anticipate changes in the weather, while aquatic insects can judge their depth from the water pressure.

Would you believe?

• Victorian street entertainers used to "train" fleas to perform in Flea Circuses. The insects performed incredible balancing feats on tiny tightropes and trapezes. They were not taught how to do this, as their natural sense of balance enabled them to do the tricks. They were harnessed by twists of thin wire to prevent escape, fed on the "trainer's" arm, and easily replaced if they refused to perform.
• Honeybees can measure their flight speed by means of long hairs that protrude between the facets of their eyes. The bee senses how much these hairs are bent by the air rushing past them, and thus works out its speed.

Below

The hairs of some prickly or woolly bear caterpillars break to release irritant substances – so don't touch!

Bristle

Socket

Cuticle

Left

A highly enlarged bristle and its nerve-rich socket in the exoskeleton.

Sensory nerve

Amazing Antennae

Bugs use their antennae for touch, smell, and taste – and some can hear with them, too!

Nearly all adult insects have two finger-like "feelers" or antennae protruding from the head, usually between or in front of the compound eyes. They are vital, multisensitive parts that tell an insect an enormous amount about the surroundings. The antennal surface is thick with minute hairs, pegs, knobs, bristles, and scales that are sensitive to odors and chemicals, movements, physical contact, and even air humidity.

Their main function is usually smell and/or taste (as described on the following page). Bugs often wave their antennae about as they "sniff" the air for tell-tale smells, scents, and odors.

Above

This antenna from a ladybug has been magnified 95 times to reveal patterns of tiny hairs, bumps, and pits where the microreceptors for smell and taste are.

Long and short

Antennae are usually segmented tubes, moved by tiny muscles inside (like the legs). They vary tremendously in size and shape among insect species. They may be tubular, tapering, thread-like, short, bristle-shaped, or filamentous, and much longer than the insect's entire body. They tend to be shorter in day-active insects that can see well, like dragonflies, and longer in insects that "feel" their way in darkness. The longest-known antennae belong to a type of Nigerian cave cricket (*Phaeophilacris*), which is nearly blind.

ANTENNAE SHAPES AND SIZES

Design	Insect group	Insect
Elbowed	Hymenoptera	Ant
Aristate	Hymenoptera	Wasp
Thread-like	Orthoptera	Grasshopper
Clubbed	Coleoptera	Carrion beetle
Feathery	Lepidoptera	Moth
Comb-like	Coleoptera	Cockchafer
Saw-like	Mantodea	Mantis
Beaded	Coleoptera	Blister beetle
Bristle-like	Plecoptera	Stonefly
Inconspicuous	Odonata	Dragonfly

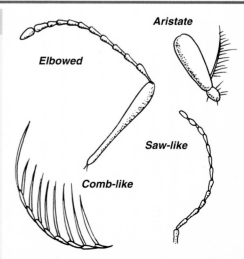

Elbowed

Aristate

Saw-like

Comb-like

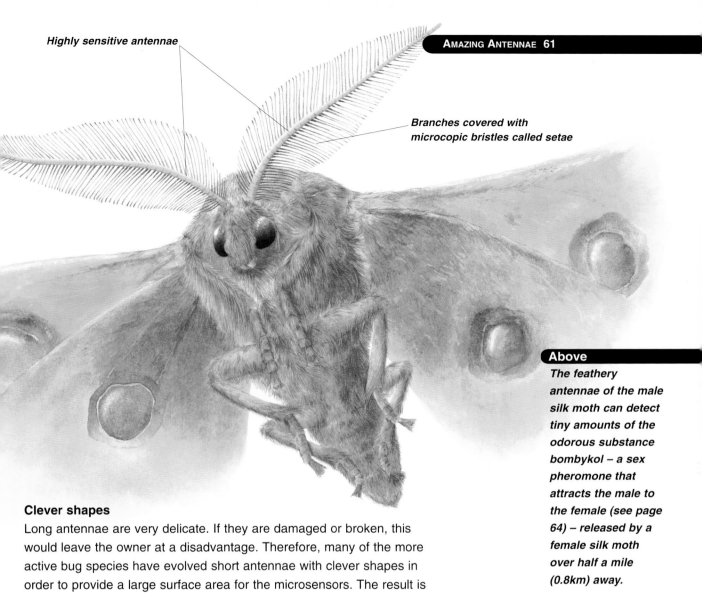

Highly sensitive antennae

Branches covered with
microcopic bristles called setae

Above
*The feathery
antennae of the male
silk moth can detect
tiny amounts of the
odorous substance
bombykol – a sex
pheromone that
attracts the male to
the female (see page
64) – released by a
female silk moth
over half a mile
(0.8km) away.*

Clever shapes

Long antennae are very delicate. If they are damaged or broken, this
would leave the owner at a disadvantage. Therefore, many of the more
active bug species have evolved short antennae with clever shapes in
order to provide a large surface area for the microsensors. The result is
a huge variety of antennae designs (see panel).

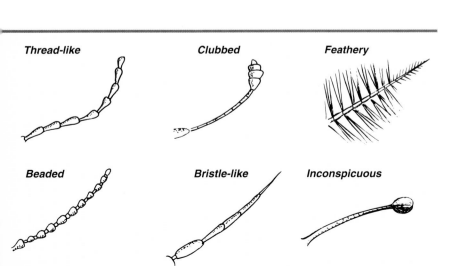

Thread-like

Clubbed

Feathery

Beaded

Bristle-like

Inconspicuous

Would you believe?

A drone honeybee
has 30,000 smell or
olfactory receptors on an
antenna only 1/4 in.
(6mm) long!

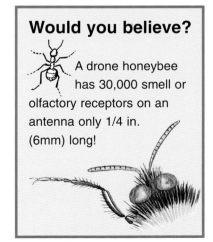

Smell and Taste

Many insects live in a world dominated by smells and tastes, rather than by lights and sounds.

Some insects have impressive sight and hearing, but their olfaction – or sense of smell – is even more outstanding. We cannot comprehend the complexity of the messages they read from chemical odorants floating in the air. Bugs use smell to communicate, orientate, navigate, detect humidity, find food and water, locate suitable egg-laying sites, and identify friends and foes.

Smelly organs

The insect's olfactory receptors, also called chemoreceptors, are porous pegs or cones covered by a very thin layer of cuticle, and containing sensory nerve cells. They are usually concentrated on the antennae (shown on the previous page), though there may be some on the mouth parts too. Insects constantly wave their antennae, sweeping the air for scent molecules, which they can detect in the most minute quantities.

Above

Like all animals, insects need water to stay alive. Butterflies crowd around a puddle to drink, testing the flavor with their feet. They may even congregate around pools of animal urine, which contains certain minerals and salts that they need.

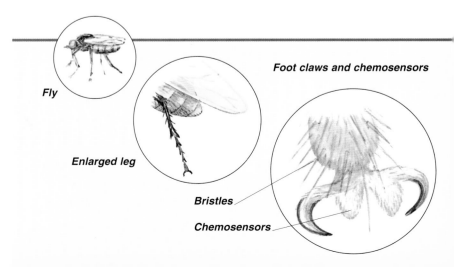

Fly

Enlarged leg

Foot claws and chemosensors

Bristles

Chemosensors

Tasty parts

Insects rely on taste, as well as smell, to determine whether foods are suitable to eat. Taste receptors are similar in structure and function to olfactory receptors. Both detect the presence of various chemicals – airborne in smell, and by contact in taste.

Taste or gustatory receptors are usually found only on and around the mouth parts. Some insects have them on the antennae, and certain bees, butterflies, and flies have them on their feet too. Some female crickets and wasps can taste with their egg-laying tube or ovipositor, using it to identify a suitable substance for the eggs.

Four flavors

Insects are sensitive to the same four basic flavors as we are: sweet, sour, salty, and bitter. However, what is a pleasant taste to us may not be pleasant to them! But we share with them a preference for sweet foods like sugar, honey, and nectar. Taste is also used by social insects for identification and communication while they groom each other.

Would you believe?

As a butterfly lands on a suitable flower, it uncoils its tube-shaped proboscis, ready to feed. This reaction is caused by an increase in its internal blood pressure, stimulated by the taste receptors on its feet! The monarch butterfly reacts to a sugar solution of only 0.0003 percent strength – more than 2,000 times more sensitive than the average human tongue!

Right

A fly approaches anything that might be food using its long-range, antenna-based sense of smell. As soon as it lands, it makes a more accurate assessment using the taste receptors on its feet. It tests the food again with its proboscis before feeding.

This enlarged view of a fly's foot shows how it is covered with sensory bristles. Some of these respond to touch, but most are devoted to taste.

Communicating by Scents

Insects communicate using pheromones – relatively simple chemicals that are spread in the air and by touch.

Pheromones are chemical substances released by the sending animal that cause a certain response or behavior in the receiver – usually an individual of the same species. There are hundreds of kinds of insect pheromones, and they dominate many aspects of their life, especially among social insects.

Pheromones are produced in specialized glands and stored, ready for instant use. They are released into the air or onto objects through specialized, hair-like setae that act as wicks. The receiver detects them by smell, and sometimes by taste, too.

A multitude of scents
• Sex pheromones, sometimes called attractants, are usually released by females to trigger courtship and mating by males.
• Alarm pheromones, used mainly by social insects, stimulate escape or defensive behavior. They are highly volatile and soon fade, so the message spreads rapidly but does not linger once the danger is over.
• Aggregation pheromones serve to call members of a species together, for example, to a rich food source or a suitable egg-laying site. Several beetle species (especially bark beetles), cockroaches, and solitary and social bees and wasps, employ such scents.

• Dispersal pheromones have the opposite effect, driving individuals away to reduce competition between them. The female apple-maggot fly applies this pheromone to fruit after she has laid an egg in it. This reduces the likelihood of another female doing the same, so ensuring her offspring have plenty of food.

• Trail pheromones are employed by ants and termites, to lay a scent trail to food. This is why ants slavishly seem to follow an invisible path – they are detecting the pheromone with their antennae. At moving time, scouts leave trail pheromones to guide the colony to a suitable, new nest site.

Below

In some butterflies, sex pheromones are produced by special scent-scales on the hindwings of the males. They are scattered into the air by "brushes" on the front wings and serve to attract females.

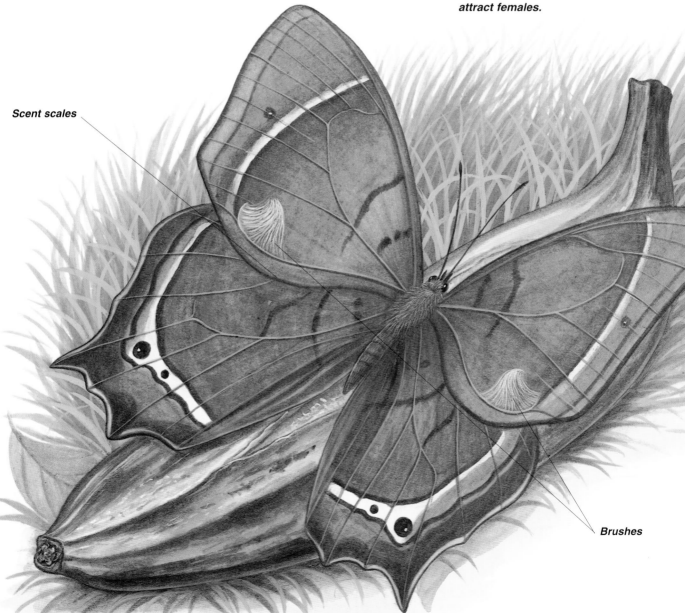

Scent scales

Brushes

How Insects Behave

Insect behavior is based on combinations of fixed patterns, called instincts.

Behavior – what animals do in response to certain situations – has two main sources. One is an array of inbuilt or inherited behavior patterns called instincts. The other is learned experiences, accumulated by trial and error through the animal's life.

Most insect behavior is instinctive. It's a complex combination of rigid, stereotyped actions and patterns, governed by the genes and usually identical in every member of the species. A few insects can learn new types of behavior in the light of experience. But whether they consciously make decisions like us is very doubtful indeed!

Changing instincts

Instinct is one of the many reasons for insect success. Over a long time and many generations, it can be fine tuned by evolution. Behavior is subject to natural selection, just like the shape of a wing or leg.

Above

This female sand-wasp catches a large caterpillar, paralyzes it, and then drags it to her burrow, where she will tear and eat it. All of these movements are instinctive, based on built-in behavior patterns derived from the bug's genes.

LEARNING BY HABITUATION

Fruit or vinegar flies (*Drosophila*) are normally attracted by the scents of rotting fruit, and repelled by odors such as peppermint. However, in experiments, if they are exposed to peppermint throughout their larval stages, they become used to it, or habituated. They may even be attracted by it!

New, instinctive behavior patterns crop up occasionally when genes are altered by the natural process of mutation. If the change is unhelpful, it's weeded out by natural selection. If the change is beneficial, the individuals possessing it survive and breed more successfully. So the new, instinctive behavior spreads through the species.

Learning

Instinctive behavior can be modified to cope with changing situations by learning. Insects have a limited ability to learn, usually by habituation or association. Habituation is developing new behavior after long-term exposure to certain conditions (see panel). Association involves learning by trial and error (see other panel).

Biological clocks

Most animals have regular or rhythmic behavior governed by an internal "biological clock" in the brain. Insects are no exception:
• Foraging insects need to know when their food flowers are due to open and produce nectar.
• Bees can be trained to come to a feeder at a precise time of day.
• Fireflies flash only at certain times in the 24-hour cycle, even when kept in constant darkness.

LEARNING BY TRIAL AND ERROR

This experiment uses glass dishes on colored-paper squares. One dish, on the blue square, contains a sugar solution. The others only have water. Honeybees investigate the dishes, find the sugary one by trial and error, and associate it with the color. Then they can remember where to return for some sweet food. But they continue to return to the blue dish, even when the sugar solution is replaced by plain water. So they are not very clever!

Would you believe?

Digger wasps memorize landmarks around their burrows so that they can return after feeding trips. You can trick them by moving the landmarks. Place a circle of fir cones around the entrance to a wasp's burrow. The wasp flies around the cones and inspects them, learning the new scene, before it goes off to feed. Now move the circle of cones away from the hole. When the wasp returns, it flies straight to the center of the cone circle – but there's no burrow entrance! (Put the cones back, of course.)

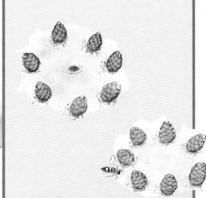

Body Language

Insects often communicate with body language, using postures, positions, and actions to inform each other.

Many insects use their senses, especially sight and touch, to assess the postures and movements of their fellows. So body language, including displays and dances, is an important method of communication when finding a mate, challenging a rival, or passing on information.

Courting time

Courtship dances are very species-specific. They help an insect to identify a member of its own species and make sure it is of the opposite sex, to save wasted time! At breeding time, rival males often go into ritual postures and movements to show their superiority and impress the females. The females, in turn, have more subtle courtship gestures to signify their moods and intents.

Above

Wild bees bustle about on the side of the comb, waiting for scouts to return with information. As the many scouts return, they compare dances and head off to the best food source.

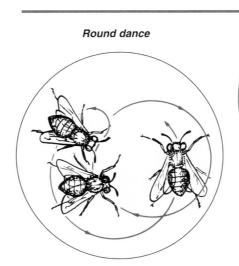

Round dance

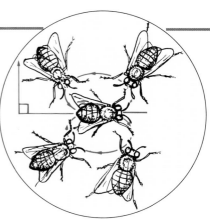

Waggle dance

Dance ⟶

Angle of sun ⟶

Dancing bees

The most famous example of insect body language is the dance of the worker honeybee. The workers pass information to each other about food and water sources by a series of ritual movements. These are performed in the dark hive, on the vertical surfaces of wax honeycombs.

The dancer is usually a worker who has discovered a new source of nectar, pollen, or water. She communicates the distance, direction, and nutritional value of the food by her movements (see panel). "Followers" crowd around and analyze her movements with their antennae. She usually brings back a sample of the food and the others beg for a taste, to learn its type and the flower's scent. The dancing excites the followers and encourages them to visit the food.

Would you believe?

Bee dances and body language were discovered by German zoologist Karl von Frisch in 1944. He watched the bees' responses as he moved food sources around their hive. Later research found that different strains of honeybee from around the world have "dance dialects" – slightly different versions of the same basic dance movements.

Left

Worker bees prepare to leave the hive on scouting expeditions early in the day. They find flowers by sight and scent, and return to dance on the combs if they contain pollen and nectar.

WHAT THE BEE'S DANCE MEANS

• Round dance – when the food is within about 27 yds. (25m).
The more frequently she changes direction, the greater the nutritional value of the food.
• Hybrid of round and waggle dances – the food is between 27–110 yds. (25–100m).
• Waggle dance – the food is more than about 110 yds. (100m) away.
The dance is a series of figures-of-eight. The length of the straight run and the number of times she waggles her abdomen indicates the distance. The angle of the straight run, relative to vertical, indicates the direction of the food relative to the sun as viewed from the hive. For example, a run straight up means the food is straight toward the sun. A run at 90° to the left of vertical means fly 90° (a right angle) to the left of the sun.

3

ATTACK, DEFENSE, AND FEEDING

INSECTS HAVE DEVELOPED A HUGE RANGE OF SURVIVAL
MECHANISMS TO HELP TO PROTECT THEM AGAINST OTHER ANIMALS —
FROM THEIR MOUTH PARTS TO THEIR SPEED, STRENGTH, AND
MULTIPLE DISGUISES, INCLUDING THEIR ABILITY TO "PLAY DEAD."

ALTHOUGH MOST INSECTS DEPEND ON PLANTS FOR SURVIVAL, MANY
INSECTS ARE CARNIVOROUS, AND WILL ATTACK AND EAT EVEN THEIR
OWN KIND; OTHERS, SUCH AS MOSQUITOES, ATTACK HUMANS. SOME
INSECTS ARE PARASITIC, LIVING OFF OTHER CREATURES WHO PROVIDE
THEM WITH BOTH FOOD AND SHELTER; OTHER ARE SCAVENGERS, WHO
FEED ON ROTTING ANIMALS AND PLANTS, AND THUS CONTRIBUTE TO
THE RECYCLING OF MANY NATURAL RESOURCES.

WHATEVER THEIR FOOD SOURCE, HOWEVER, INSECTS' FEEDING
HABITS ARE EXTREMELY IMPORTANT TO MAINTAINING THE STABILITY OF
THE ECOSYSTEM, AS WITHOUT THEM, WE WOULD BE DEVASTATED.

Attack, Defense, and Feeding

No animal group has more variations in these basic survival techniques than the insects.

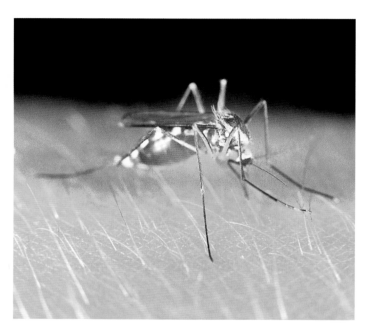

To survive, any animal needs to defend itself against would-be predators, to go on the attack when necessary, and to find enough food to eat. Insects show a dazzling array of attack-and-defense methods, and they feed on almost anything, from solid wood to rotting excrement.

Attack

Insects go on the attack for various reasons. They may be trying to kill prey for food, or to get in first during a fight with a predator, or to challenge others for mates, living space, or food sources. Many species follow our saying that "attack is the best form of defense." They use almost every body part, including mouths, limbs, feet, spines, horns, stings, and chemicals, such as poisons and irritants.

Defense

Bugs are amazingly diverse in defense. Some hide by camouflage or disguise. Others simply run away and hide, or hold their ground and use startle tactics. Still others advertise themselves with bright colors that warn: "Leave me alone, I'm poisonous or dangerous!" Some insects cheat by copying these warning colors when they are, in fact, harmless.

Bugs also employ a huge variety of chemicals in their defense, such as unpleasant tastes and smells, and acid sprays. Social insects rely on the principle of "safety in numbers," often living in fortified castles that few creatures dare to enter.

Feeding

Insects show the same basic feeding habits as other animals. There are herbivores or plant eaters, and carnivores or animal eaters, as well as detritivores or scavengers. Due to the generally small size of bugs, many are parasites and pests of larger creatures.

However, very few insects are omnivores (creatures that eat both plant and animal food). Their rigid and instinctive behavior patterns, and highly specialized mouth parts, mean that most insects can deal with only a certain type of food.

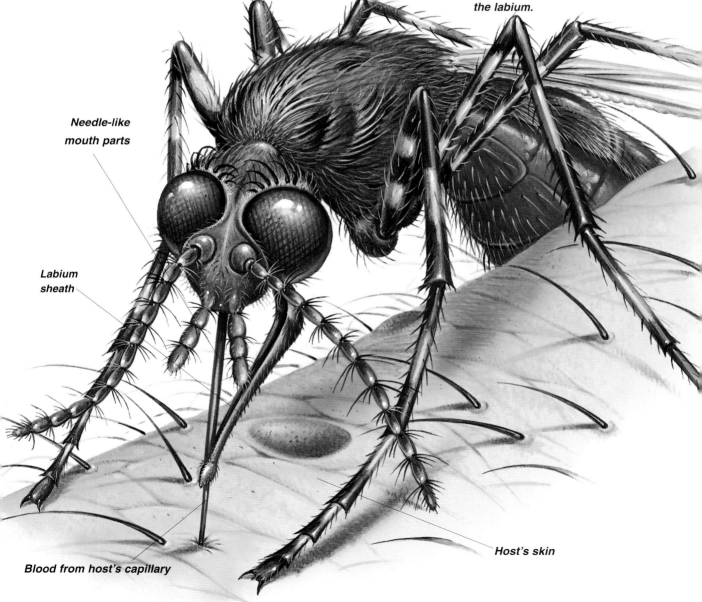

Needle-like mouth parts

Labium sheath

Blood from host's capillary

Host's skin

Adaptable Mouth Parts

Insects have a huge range of mouth parts adapted for many different foods and jobs, but all made of the same basic units.

Insects' mouth parts are jointed extensions of the exoskeleton, arranged around the mouth. The basic design is as follows:

- An upper labrum, a lip, or sheath.
- A pair of jaw-like or pincer-shaped mandibles for cutting or tearing food.
- A pair of similar maxillae for holding the food, each with a soft, sensory part called a palp to taste it.
- A lower labium, lip, or sheath, also with a pair of palps.

This basic design is adapted in various insect groups for chewing solid food, tunnelling in wood or earth, sucking up liquid food, sponging up soupy food, and piercing hard objects. Not all insects have all the mouth parts, and they vary in size and shape according to their adaptations and uses.

Eating solids

The jaw-like toothed mandibles are often the most obvious mouth parts. They move from side to side as they cut, crush, chew, and grind solid foods. The food is held firmly by the smaller maxillae and tasted by the short, sensory palps. The labium guides the food into the mouth opening itself, where it is further tasted and moved backwards by the tongue-like hypopharynx.

Above

The mantis catches its prey not with its mouth parts, but between the spine-lined second and third sections of its front legs. There is no escape from the vice-like grip as the mantis chews its impaled victim alive.

MOUTHS FOR BUGS

Chewing mandibles	Dragonflies, damselflies, grasshoppers, crickets, beetles, bees, ants
Elongated labium	Bees, to lap nectar and other fluids
Spongy labium	Housefly
Mask-like labium with jaws at end	Dragonfly nymphs
Piercing-sucking mouth parts or "beak"	True bugs, leafhoppers, treehoppers, fleas, sucking lice, some adult flies, such as mosquitoes
Siphoning mouth parts	Butterflies and moths

Right

The coconut flower weevil is a type of beetle. It chews its food with tiny jaws at the end of its long "nose" or rostrum, which is an extension of the front of the head.

The mouth parts of young and adults from the same species are often different. An adult dragonfly has the usual mandibular jaws, but its aquatic nymph grabs passing food with a pair of grasping pincers at the tip of the labium.

Drinking liquids

Sucking insects have various combinations of the usual mouth parts. They are usually elongated and formed into a tube for injecting digestive saliva into the prey and then sucking up the liquified body contents. The basic tube design may be needle sharp for piercing, blade-like for cutting, sponge-shaped for soaking and dabbing, or long and straw-like for simple sucking.

Would you believe?

Butterflies and moths have a drinking-straw mouth part called a proboscis. This is usually coiled under the head, and is straightened for sucking. Its length indicates the owner's food type. Nectar feeders have longer versions to reach inside flowers than butterflies who eat decaying fruit. The deeper or more trumpet-shaped the bloom, the longer the proboscis. The proboscis of the Madagascan sphinx moth is 10 in. (250mm) in length!

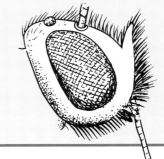

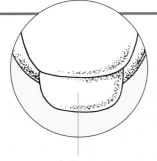

Labrum
(the upper lip; often protects the other parts)

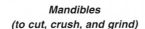

Mandibles
(to cut, crush, and grind)

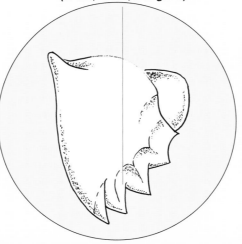

Left

Cockroaches are omnivores – they eat anything they can find. Their mouth parts, suitably, have an all-purpose design.

The Predators

Carnivorous insects employ speed, strength, surprise, disguise, stealth, and cunning to catch their victims.

The flesh-eating or carnivorous insects exploit almost every kind of animal group for food. Indeed, many are insectivores – they prey on their fellow bugs! Other common victims include small creatures, such as worms, slugs, snails, spiders, and millipedes.

The hunter's lifestyle

True hunters include members of the hemipterans (true bugs), dragonflies and damselflies, beetles, lacewings, mantids, flies, ants, and wasps. They show a range of activity. Dragonflies busily seek out and chase their prey. They need sharp senses, speed, and agility. Stalkers creep up on potential prey until close enough to attack. Mantids lie still, perhaps hidden or camouflaged, waiting to ambush a hapless victim who wanders too close. Whatever their methods, these hunters rely on a final, lightning-fast strike to capture their prey.

Above

The green tiger beetle has the long legs, strong wings, large eyes, and formidable mouth parts of a typical, active hunter.

Left

The assassin bug has no jaws. Instead, it has long, hard, spear-like stylets. It feels the victim's body with its labium to locate a thin section of cuticle between the segments, then drives in the stylets.

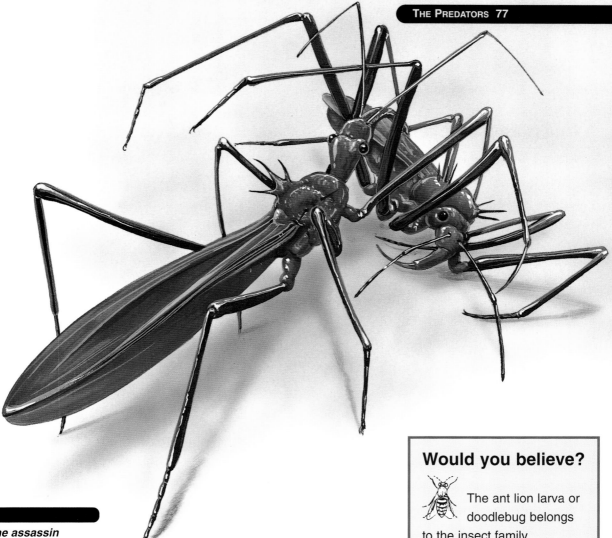

Holding food

Most predators use their large, toothed maxillae or mandibles for grabbing, holding, and then tearing up their victims. Others, especially those with piercing and sucking mouth parts for blood or body fluids, use specially adapted front legs. These insects predigest their food by injecting saliva containing digestive enzymes into the living prey. The enzymes break down and dissolve the victim's body tissues. After a time, the insect sucks up the resulting soupy liquid.

Would you believe?

The ant lion larva or doodlebug belongs to the insect family Myrmeleontidae. It digs a funnel-shaped pit in loose sand by shuffling backwards, working around in a circle, throwing sand outward with its huge head. Then it buries itself at the bottom of the pit, and waits for a small insect to tumble in. The ant lion flicks grains at the quarry as it tries to escape up the loose slope. Finally, the prey tires and slides down into the long, spiny jaws.

Parasite or Parasitoid?

A true parasite depends on its host for food and/or shelter, and thus does the host harm – but rarely kills it.

A parasite lives at the expense of another organism, the host. The parasite gains food, shelter, or some other need from the host, which suffers in the process. But often, this is not much, as it is not always in the parasite's interest to kill off its host, or eventually, its species will be doomed.

Parasitic relationships may be temporary, at a certain stage in the life cycle, or permanent. They can also be obligate, when the parasite cannot exist without a specific host, or facultative, when the parasite can use different hosts as required.

Ecto- and endo-

In fact, there are relatively few species of truly parasitic insects. Lice and fleas are external or ectoparasites, sucking the blood and body fluids from larger animals like birds and mammals. Some fly larvae, like botflies, live within their hosts and are called endoparasites.

Above

The large white caterpillar is dead, an empty husk. Wasp grubs ate its less-important organs after the caterpillar was paralyzed by a sting from their mother. They then ate its vital organs as their last meal before becoming pupae.

What's a parasitoid?

Most insects that live at the expense of other creatures are more correctly termed "parasitoids." They are somewhere in between true predators, or hunters, and true parasites. They derive sustenance from the host until the time when they can survive alone – and they usually kill the host in the process.

Most parasitoid insects lay their eggs in or on a host. The young hatch and gradually consume the victim's body as they grow. They begin by eating the tissues least vital to the host's survival, in order to keep their "living larder" alive until they reach maturity.

"Parasitic" parasitoids

The main insects to adopt the parasitoid lifestyle are the rather misnamed "parasitic" wasps of the families Ichneumonidae and Chalcididae. There are tens of thousands of species. There are also examples among flies and beetles.

Each parasitoid species tends to be restricted to a single host species or a group of closely related host species. Many chalcid and ichneumon wasps (sometimes called ichneumon flies) use caterpillars as victims. The adult females find their hosts by first seeking out the right habitat, then finding the host itself in which to lay their eggs.

As with ecto- and endoparasites, there are ecto- and endoparasitoids. The former usually complete their development during the one stage of the host's growth. In contrast, endoparasitoids often accompany their hosts as they both pass through several stages of development.

Would you believe?

 The females of a parasitic group of insects called Strepsipterans live within their hosts. The male mates with the grub-like female through a special opening on her thorax that protrudes from the host's body. The eggs then hatch inside their mother's body, killing her and her host as they grow.

Right

The human head louse is a blood-sucking ectoparasite that lives on the scalp. The female louse cements her tiny, pale eggs, commonly called "nits," to the human head hairs. Lice can spread diseases such as typhus and relapsing fever by biting someone with the disease, taking in the germs with the blood, and then injecting them into another person.

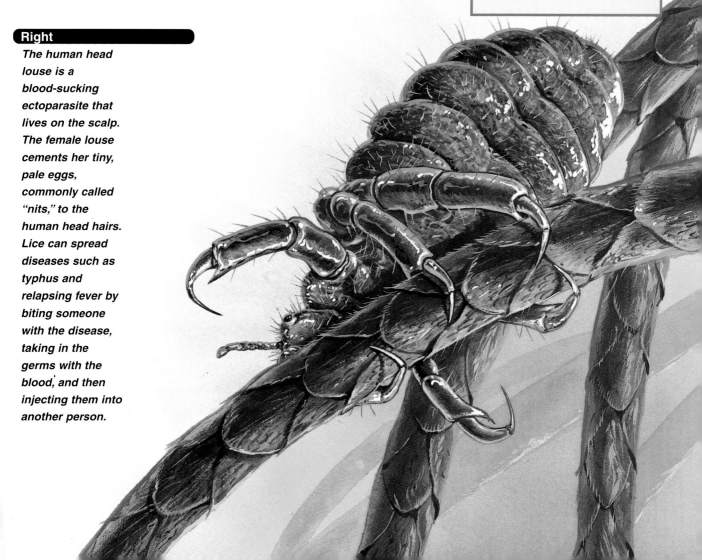

The Plant Eaters

Almost every part of every plant provides food for some insect, somewhere.

Above

Gypsy-moth caterpillars eat the leaves of almost any broad-leaved or needle-leaved tree, and they can even cause its death. When a naturalist accidentally released some of these moths in 1869, in North America, he caused one of the worst insect plagues ever.

Most herbivorous insects are fussy feeders. They depend on a single plant species, even one small part of that plant, for their food. But the female tries to make it easy for her offspring. She usually lays her eggs directly on the food plant, so the larvae hatch out onto their first meal. If they exhaust that source, it's often just a short trek to find another plant of the same kind in the same clump.

Mouths for plant parts

Plant eaters have a variety of equipment for dealing with their food (see page 74). Strong, chewing mouth parts of the wood borers can bite, chew, and masticate even hard wood. The piercing-sucking mouth parts of aphids drink plant juices and sap. Siphoning mouth parts of butterflies and moths delicately sip nectar. Chewing-lapping mouth parts are more adaptable, capable of consuming both solid and liquid foods.

Foods through life

Many insects consume different plant foods at different stages of their lives – and they have different mouth-part designs to cope at each phase. This applies especially to the caterpillars and adults of moths and butterflies. It helps to ensure that the young are not in direct competition with their parents on a food plant.

In some cases, such as the mayfly, the adults have no mouth parts at all. They cannot eat. They quickly court and mate, and soon perish.

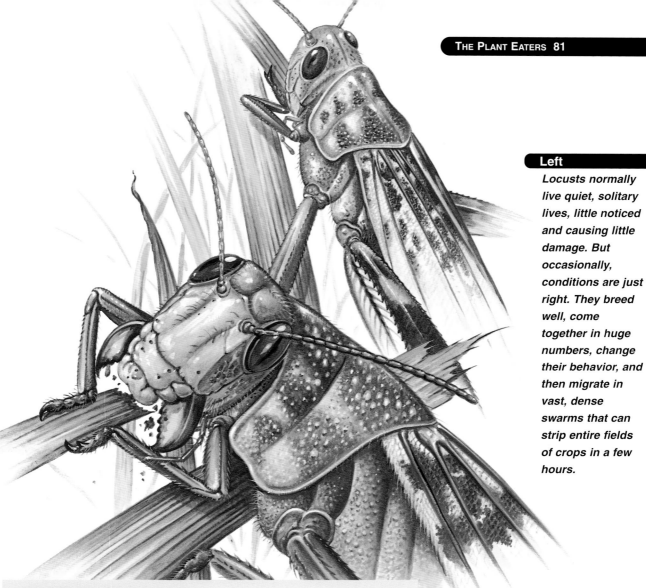

Left

Locusts normally live quiet, solitary lives, little noticed and causing little damage. But occasionally, conditions are just right. They breed well, come together in huge numbers, change their behavior, and then migrate in vast, dense swarms that can strip entire fields of crops in a few hours.

HOW INSECTS ATTACK PLANTS

No part of a plant is safe from insect attack! They attack by:
• Chewing leaves, such as the caterpillars of the cinnabar moth, oak tortrix moth, and thousands of other species.
• Leaf mining or tunnelling within the thickness of the leaf, such as the celery-fly larva.
• Piercing and sucking plant saps, such as aphids (greenfly and blackfly), leaf hoppers, and scale insects.
• Eating bark, such as the large elm-bark beetle.
• Boring through and eating the living wood, such as the larvae of the furniture beetle ("woodworms") and deathwatch beetle.
• Eating the nuts, berries, fruits, and other seeds, such as the nut weevil and apple-codling moth.
• Feeding on and in the roots, such as cranefly larvae ("leatherjackets") in grassy meadows.
• Consuming the fungus that grows on old or dead plants, such as the fungus gnat.
• Existing on dead and rotting wood, such as the stag-beetle larva.

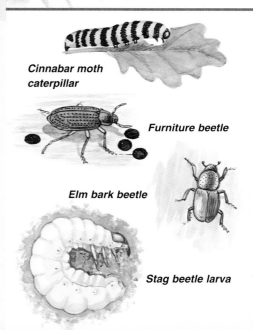

Cinnabar moth caterpillar

Furniture beetle

Elm bark beetle

Stag beetle larva

The Scavengers

Insect scavengers rid the world of wastes, freeing the nutrients and recycling them back into the food chains.

Scavenging insects feed mainly on the bits and bodies of creatures, plants, and fungi that are dead, and perhaps rotting away. Some specialize on animal droppings, wastes, and dung. Most of these scavengers have chewing or sponging mouth parts. They are not picky eaters, accepting whatever is available. However, some, like ants, prefer sweeter foods.

A rotten world

Insect scavengers, or detritivores, are found everywhere. The leaf litter of the forest floor and the soil beneath teem with untold millions of beetles and fly larvae, feeding on rotting plant material.

A dead animal's body is rapidly consumed by a whole series of flesh-eating flies and their maggots, carrion and other beetle grubs. Experts can date the death of a body – including a human body – from the well-recognized order in which these various insect species feed on it, over hours, days, and weeks.

Meanwhile, the carcass gradually sinks into the ground due to the efforts of large burying beetles beneath, who provide a moist food store of flesh for their young. When all the soft tissues have gone, the dry skin and bones are finished off by yet more beetles.

The insects that consume the dry skin, fur and feathers include the dreaded museum beetle, the scourge of natural history collections, the clothes moth, less of a problem in these days of synthetic fabrics, and the carpet beetle, which will eat any fibers, natural or manmade.

Above

Bark-beetle larvae or grubs burrow beneath tree bark, eating the soft, nutritious layer until they emerge as mature adults. As they fly from tree to tree, they carry bacteria and viruses. Elm-bark beetles, for example, spread Dutch elm disease in the 1970s, which devastated many trees.

Termites are indispensable to the natural world, as they break down dead trees, recycle the nutrients, and create space for new growth. But in the human world, they destroy wooden structures such as buildings, floors, roofs, bridges, dams, and furniture.

Yummy dung

Insects that feed on dung are true specialists. Every dropping and pat seethes with its own population of flies and beetles. Many of these are specific to the animal who provided the food, such as a zebra, horse, rhino, or elephant. Scarab beetles roll away balls of fresh, moist dung and bury them, laying their eggs on the smelly lump that will be food for their young.

Scavengers at sea

The ultimate in specialized scavenging are the ocean striders, sea-faring versions of pond skaters. They live on the surface of the sea, many miles from land, where the currents bring together floating mats of trash. The insects feed on the carcasses of drowned insects and sea birds.

Would you believe?

 Termites destroy trees and wooden structures – yet they cannot actually digest wood! They have no digestive enzymes for plant cellulose, the chief component of wood. The termites rely on friendly microbes living within their guts to produce enzymes to attack the cellulose.

Fruit flies, as their name suggests, enjoy fruit. The smell of ripe fruit, such as this orange, attracts them, and they congregate to feed on the sweet juices and to mate. They will lay eggs here too, so that their grubs will have a ready food source.

Defense Strategies

Most insects are relatively small, so they need to defend themselves against their many, larger predators.

If an attacker loses concentration for a split second, the victim may get away. This is how many insects defend themselves – by escape, using speed and perhaps diversion tactics. They may fly away in an instant, like houseflies, or leap away, like grasshoppers and crickets, or run swiftly for cover, like cockroaches and ground beetles.

If caught by a leg, some insects may sacrifice the limb using an "autoamputation" mechanism at its joint with the body. Special muscles contract to shear the joint and seal the wound against bleeding and infection.

The click beetle arches its body at a loosely hinged joint between its prothorax and the rest of its body before throwing itself into the air. It then flexes suddenly in the opposite direction, snapping a spine-like extension of the front of the sternum into a snug-fitting groove at the rear, thus making the "click."

Wow! What was that?
Numerous insects use startle or surprise tactics to distract the predator and gain a valuable second. They include the noisy takeoffs of click beetles and band-winged grasshoppers. The grasshopper suddenly leaps, spreads its wings to reveal their bold-colored patterns ... then the patterns disappear as the insect folds its wings and drops to the ground, apparently vanishing in midair!

Giant eyes
In nature, the large eyes of a predator, such as a cat or snake, are a feared sight. Many large insects, like giant silk moths, have huge "eyespots" on their wings, normally hidden when resting. When disturbed, the moth moves its wings and flashes the great eyes.

Eyespots also serve to direct an attack away from vital parts of the body. This type of defense is called target presentation. Some caterpillars have false eyes and head markings on their rear ends, which are less vital than the real head if attacked.

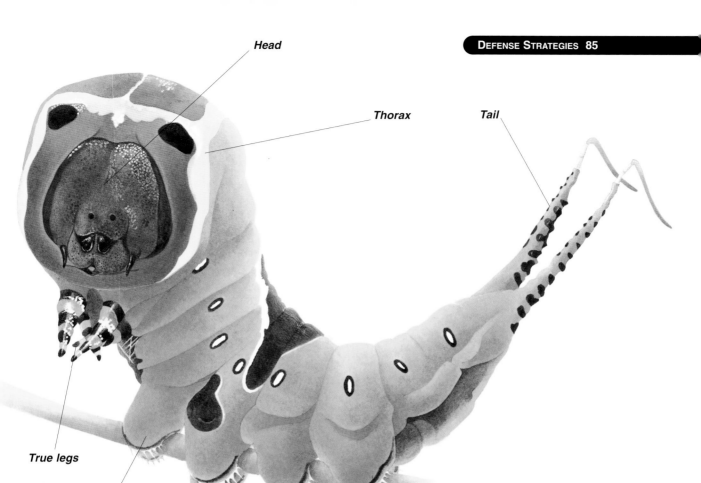

Head

Thorax

Tail

True legs

Prolegs

Concealment

Insects are small and hide easily. Countless bugs simply live beneath rocks, stumps, in forest leaf litter, and in the soil. Others, such as the young of wood-boring beetles, leaf miners and gall wasps are concealed within their food. Spittlebug or froghopper nymphs (family Cercopidae) create frothy masses in which to hide. Insects are also supreme at camouflage and disguise, as shown on the following pages.

Playing dead

Many insects use the effective defense of "playing dead." Most animal hunters rely on detecting the movements of their prey, so they simply cannot find an immobile insect, especially in camouflage colors. Giant water bugs (family Belostomatidae) may feign death for 15 minutes or more when removed from the water.

Above

A newly molted puss-moth caterpillar rears up in threatening pose. Pulling its head in, it swells the thorax region, revealing bright red markings and eyespots. Two long, red, whip-shaped tails appear and wave menacingly over its head. And it's not an empty threat – this caterpillar can spray acid at its attacker!

Color and Pattern

Insects display some of nature's most brilliant colors – but their motive is survival, not beauty.

Insects use colors and patterns for many reasons: to camouflage, disguise, warn, startle, outshine rivals, court mates, and defend territory. Each of these topics is covered on the following pages.

The coloring substances or pigments are contained within the insect's "skin," the hard cuticle, as it forms. This means the colors and patterns can be changed at each molt if necessary, to fit with a changing lifestyle. The pigments absorb some of the colors that make up the spectrum or rainbow within white light, and reflect the others. So a red insect has pigments that absorb all colors, except red.

Above

The bright colors of these Australian shieldbugs advertise the fact that their flesh tastes extremely unpleasant.

Colors from foods

The most common pigments are blacks (which absorb nearly all light), grays, browns, reds, yellows, and dull greens. They may be manufactured within the insect's body or absorbed from the food it eats. For example, the green color of many leaf-eating insects comes from the green plant pigment chlorophyll, which is found in the foliage they consume. Ladybugs get their red and yellow pigments from substances called flavones in their prey.

PIGMENT TYPES

Hundreds of pigments are used by insects. Here are a few from the butterfly group:

Black, gray, brown	Cream and yellow	White	Yellow
melanin produced by the insect's body	flavones from plant leaves	leucopterin, derived from uric acid (a common byproduct of animal body chemistry)	xanthopterin, derived from uric acid

The cuticle of this dogbane-leaf beetle has the structural color of black, with the pigment melanin. The optical colors of the iridescent sheen are produced by microscopic ridges, like those on the surface of a compact disc (CD), which scatter the light in different directions.

Shimmering hues

The normal, pigmented cuticle produces what are called structural colors. Some insects also have minute, transparent or translucent, scale-like structures on the cuticle, or ultrafine layers, blocks, or raised ridges. These work like tiny mirrors and lenses to bend and diffuse light. They produce optical colors – dazzling, iridescent hues, such as shimmering, metallic blues, violets, whites, and greens, which change as the insect moves.

STRUCTURAL OR OPTICAL?

• If the insect is dry and then wetted, structural colors do not alter. But optical colors alter, and may even disappear if the insect is underwater.
• Structural colors appear the same, no matter what the angle of view. Optical colors change as you view the insect from different angles.

Orange	*Red*	*Green*	*Metallic blues, violets, and greens*
chrysopterin, derived from uric acid	erythropterin, derived from uric acid	pigments derived from chlorophyll, the substance that plants use to trap light energy	optical colors produced by various designs of the ridged cuticle

Would you believe?

The patterns on butterfly and moth wings are made by mosaics of minute scales arranged like tiles on a house roof. There may be 10,000 scales on one wing. Each is shaped like a table-tennis bat, with the "handle" fitted into a tiny socket. The scales are colored with pigments or covered with light-diffracting ridges. They easily dislodge as the butterfly brushes against objects, and fall off as fine dust.

Camouflage

Cryptic coloration lets insects "hide" by making them look like something of little interest to a predator.

Camouflage is blending in with the background. One major aspect is cryptic coloration, enabling insects to merge with their surroundings. Thousands of insect species are green or brown, so they can hide among leaves and twigs. Desert insects may be tawny or yellow. Those living in dark earth are themselves dark brown or black.

Pattern

The deception can be improved by avoiding areas of plain, unvarying color. Some insects have patterns and details such as wrinkles, spots, and holes that mimic patterns in nature, such as torn leaves and broken twigs.

Above

The swallowtail caterpillar gives a convincing impression of a fresh bird-dropping, with its murky coloring and knobbly shape.

Body shape and movement

The shape of the body, wings, and legs improves the disguise still further. The stick-and-leaf insects (phasmids) are masters at this sort of trickery. Their legs are twigs and their wings are leaves. Another feature is movement. The insect sways with the surroundings, copying the effects of the breeze, to complete the effect.

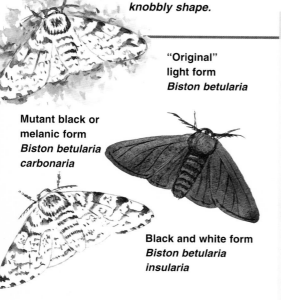

"Original"
light form
Biston betularia

Mutant black or
melanic form
Biston betularia
carbonaria

Black and white form
Biston betularia
insularia

EVOLUTION IN ACTION

Evolution normally works very slowly. But some examples among insects happen in years, rather than millennia – especially when helped by human interference.

The natural form of the peppered moth is white with pale-black spots. It is camouflaged to rest on pale, lichen-encrusted tree bark.

Occasionally, natural mutant forms, which are black or black with white spots, crop up. But they are easy for predatory birds to spot on the pale tree trunks, and they rarely survive to breed.

During the Industrial Revolution of the 18th and 19th centuries, trees near cities became coated with soot. This made the white-peppered moths an easy target on the dark tree trunks, while the mutant, dark forms were better camouflaged. Gradually, the latter became more common.

Today, the dark or melanic forms of peppered moth are still more common in cities, while the lighter forms thrive in the countryside.

"Cuckoo spit" conceals a plant-hopper nymph. This tiny insect produces the frothy liquid so it can suck up the plant's juices, live and grow, and pass through its life cycle unnoticed. If the froth is removed, the bug leaps or hops away.

Some insects opt for a more specific disguise. They resemble something that is of no interest to a predator. Many treehoppers look like thorns; some caterpillars curl up to resemble bird droppings; and various beetles or butterflies look like dead, curled-up leaves or gnarled bits of bark.

Flashing colors

Some cryptic moths and butterflies employ another strategy if their disguise fails. They momentarily spread their wings, uncovering a bright array of colors. The short, startling display distracts or frightens the predator long enough for the moth to resume its camouflage and escape.

Another type of crypsis is disruptive coloration. Large, bold patches of contrasting colors over the body break up an animal's outline, so its identity and body shape are difficult to discern. Zebras have this patterning. On a smaller scale, so do many moths, butterflies, and beetles.

Would you believe?

Many insects adopt unnatural poses to confuse their predators.

• Certain moths sit on branches with their bodies twisted sideways to resemble battered, dead leaves.

• Several beetle species lie on their sides, with odd legs and antennae sticking out at abnormal angles, to look like bird droppings.

• Stinkbug nymphs line up around their egg cases and collectively mimic a large, poisonous caterpillar.

Warners and Mimics

Insects use certain bright colors to warn that they are poisonous or taste terrible.

Bright, bold, warning colors in vivid, unmistakable patterns are used by certain creatures throughout the animal kingdom, from worms and insects to frogs and snakes. They may seem to display an easily seen, inviting target for predators, but the first-time attacker finds out that the prey has an awful smell or taste, or that its flesh is poisonous or toxic. The predator remembers such a terrible experience and learns to avoid these so-called warning colors and patterns in future.

Red for danger

Many kinds of creatures use black with bright reds, yellows, or oranges, often as spots or stripes. They include insects such as wasps, bees, and beetles like ladybugs. They all tend to benefit from this similarity and shared color codes.

The close resemblance in color and pattern between unappetizing animals is called Müllerian mimicry. One or two individuals may be injured or killed as a young predator learns the warning, but a whole range of species benefits from their sacrifice.

Above

The bright-orange and black of the monarch butterfly (Danaus plexippus) warns that its flesh contains poisonous substances or toxins. These were taken in when it was a caterpillar feeding on milkweed. The monarch is the model for the viceroy butterfly (Limenitis archippus), which is harmless – but mimics the monarch almost perfectly.

WARNING COLORS AND PATTERNS

Red and black	Yellow and black	Orange and black
cinnabar moths, ladybugs, fungus beetles, black widow spiders, tropical millipedes, fire-bellied toads, coral snakes	cinnabar moth caterpillars, arrow-poison frogs, wasps, hornets, honeybees, Colorado beetles, bombardier beetles, wasp beetles. Clear-wing moths and hoverflies are mimics!	pajama sea slugs, monarch butterflies, hornet wasps

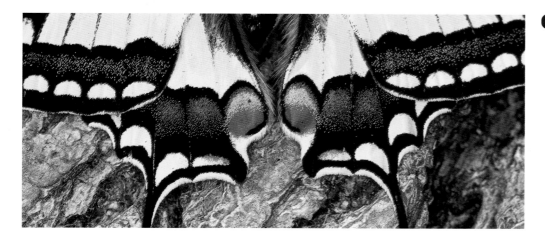

Left

The wings of the beautiful swallowtail butterfly (Papilio machaon) are brightly patterned to give the illusion that the insect is back-to-front. The hind wings have two large, red eyespots near their ends on both the upper and lower surfaces. The two "tails", for which these butterflies are named, look like antennae. A predator such as a bird will deludedly peck at the hind wings, while the real insect escapes.

False warning

Some insects that are not horrible tasting or poisonous also use warning colors to get the same protection. This trick is called Batesian mimicry. The truly bad-tasting species is the model, and the good-tasting copy-cheat is the mimic. Evolution has produced some uncanny insect mimics, especially among the butterflies.

But the system can support only a limited number of cheats. As the good-tasting mimics become more common, predators encounter the harmful models less often. So, the predators are less likely to become ill or poisoned, and less likely to learn the warning. In most cases, nature has arrived at a balance between models and mimics.

Hornet moth

Hornet

Left

In Batesian mimicry, the model and mimic do not need to be closely related, but they must live in the same area at the same season, or predators would not encounter both! The hornet with its sting and the harmless hornet moth both fly near the same trees during the summer months.

Would you believe?

• Müllerian mimicry was described by the German insect expert Fritz Müller in 1879.

• Batesian mimicry was discovered by the English naturalist Henry Walter Bates in 1861, among butterflies of the Amazon rainforests.

Chemical Warfare

Insects employ foul-smelling, stinging, or caustic chemicals to repel their enemies.

Any attacker ignores at its peril the warning colors and threat displays of insects. These are usually a means of advertising another, more powerful form of defense – the ability to bite or sting, or to ooze or spray noxious chemicals.

Smell, sick, and spray

Insects produce a range of unpleasant liquids to deter predators. Stinkbugs (family Pentatomidae) make repellent odors. Grasshoppers can regurgitate their gut contents. Ground beetles (*Anthia*) and ants squirt or spray jets of stinging formic acid. Blister beetles (family Meloidae) give off an irritant chemical, cantharidin, which causes skin blisters and sores.

Last-ditch defense

Bites and stings are normally the last line of defense for bugs, because they involve dangerous physical contact. Insects, being small, run the risk of coming off worse. Ants and many others bite with their jaws. Often the mandibles jab an irritant or poison into the wound. Ants can also squirt formic acid from the tail.

Colony-dwelling species release alarm pheromones (see page 64) when threatened, promoting a mass attack on the intruder. And bugs with piercing and sucking mouth parts also use them to give a bite that's not venomous, but painful. Pond skaters and water beetles have a nasty bite.

Above

With a sound like a gunshot, the bombardier beetle (Brachinus crepitans) squirts a hot, irritating liquid at its attacker.

Attacker

Boiling chemical mixture

Left

The bombardier beetle stores chemicals separately in its abdominal chambers. When the beetle is threatened, these mix together, causing a violent reaction as the boiling mixture explodes with a noxious puff.

Would you believe?

• Wasps and bees inject painful poisons with their stings in order to defend themselves and their colonies. But the bee-eater bird has developed a way of quickly biting off the stings before eating the insects.

• Certain birds seem to be immune to the poisons of some insects. The grosbeak feeds happily on heaps of poisonous, monarch butterfly bodies without experiencing any side effects.

• The oriole also feeds on monarch bodies, but only eats those butterflies containing less poison.

• Lubber grasshoppers emit a poisonous, foul-smelling spray, delivered with a loud, hissing sound. However, the loggerhead shrike, undeterrred, impales the grasshoppers on thorns, leaving them alone until both smell and poison have faded.

Stings

Certain moth and butterfly caterpillars – "woolly bears" – are covered with long hairs. They may look cute, but don't touch them – their hairs break to release stinging or irritating chemicals.

Many bees and wasps can jab attackers with their venomous stings. The barbed sting is a specialized ovipositor or egg-laying tube. A wasp can sting repeatedly, but a bee's sting is torn from its body and stays in its victim.

Avoiding Bad Conditions

Insects avoid hardship in two ways. They either move away, or go into a dormant, inactive state.

True migration is a yearly or seasonal movement to avoid bad conditions. It uses up a lot of energy, and exposes the animal to dangers. Insects are generally too small to survive these risks, so few insects undergo true migrations.

However, there are plenty of insect mass movements – usually for the purpose of spreading out or dispersal. This prevents competition in one place for food and shelter; reduces the risk of transferring diseases in crowded conditions; and lowers the likelihood of inbreeding within the local population.

In the fall, adult monarchs in eastern North America migrate to winter roosts in the mountain pine forests of northern central Mexico. In the west, they fly to several sites in California.

Surviving as eggs

Most insect species pass through difficult times, like extreme heat, cold, or drought, in a "sleeping" condition or stage of the life cycle. In most temperate regions, the adults lay eggs in late summer or autumn, and die with the first heavy frosts. Nevertheless, the tough eggs are able to endure the winter cold and ice. They are laid in safe, sheltered places, and the embryo's development is delayed until conditions improve and they are able to hatch successfully in the warmth of spring.

Winter "holidays"

Other insects spend the winter as larvae, pupae, or even adults. They find a sheltered spot and go into an inactive state called torpor, or hibernation. A natural antifreeze in the blood prevents their bodies from freezing solid.

In warm climates, many bugs resort to a similar dormant state, called aestivation, to survive the heat and dryness. Aquatic insects seek shelter in the mud on the bottoms of ponds and rivers. Insects like houseflies (*Musca domestica*) spend winter as adults, in the comfort of human dwellings.

Above

Adult ladybugs hibernate together in any sheltered place. The packed group protects most of the individuals from the worst of the weather, and also from predators.

HOW FAR DO THEY MIGRATE?

On the yearly, two-way journey there and back, migration distances are:

Desert locusts 2,000 miles (3,200km)

Monarchs 3,700 miles (6,000km)

Swallows 7,400 miles (12,000 km)

Gray whales 12,500 miles (20,000km)

Arctic terns 18,500 miles (30,000km)

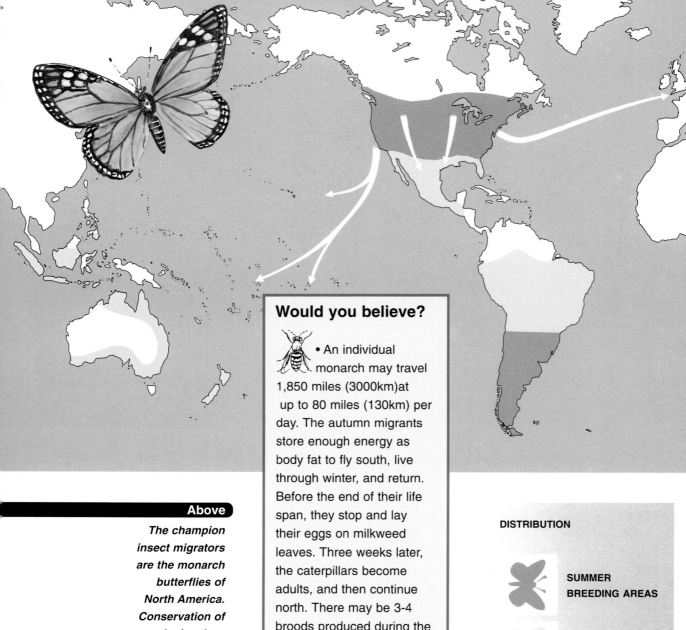

Would you believe?

• An individual monarch may travel 1,850 miles (3000km) at up to 80 miles (130km) per day. The autumn migrants store enough energy as body fat to fly south, live through winter, and return. Before the end of their life span, they stop and lay their eggs on milkweed leaves. Three weeks later, the caterpillars become adults, and then continue north. There may be 3-4 broods produced during the return trip, and these new adults make the entire southward journey in the fall, purely by instinct.

• In the winter of 1982-1983, a monarch roost in El Rosario, Mexico, covered 12 acres (5 hectares) – an area bigger than 20 football fields!

DISTRIBUTION

SUMMER
BREEDING AREAS

WINTERING
AREAS

AREAS WHERE
MONARCH
SOMETIMES SEEN

Left

In parts of northern North America, zebra swallowtails appear to be breeding residents, but they are non-breeding migrants. Conditions are not favorable so they rarely survive.

Population explosions

In temperate lands with marked seasonal changes, such as Europe, North America, and Australia, insects sometimes undergo irruptions. An irruption is a sudden change in population numbers in a particular area. It happens in some insect species (and other animals too) when the weather, food supplies and other conditions have been very favorable for weeks, months, perhaps years. This results in a population build-up, and with fast-breeding insects even a population explosion. Eventually the number of individuals becomes so large that the area cannot support them, and thousands or millions set off to find a new area. Locust irruptions are infamous. So are ladybug irruptions, when they seem to fall from the sky like raindrops, so hungry that they nibble at human skin. In Australia, millions of bogong moths may even fly out to sea.

Several kinds of butterflies also undergo irruptions, such as the mourning cloak, also called the Camberwell beauty. This fast-flying, maroon-winged nymphalid butterfly is one of the first to become active in spring, after over-wintering as an adult. It is widespread around the Northern Hemisphere, including Asia, Japan, North America and mainland Europe, but is no longer resident in Britain.

Below

The Camberwell beauty was first recorded for science in 1748, in the then-village of Camberwell, now absorbed as a suburb of south London, England. It is also called the mourning cloak.

Social Insects

Living together has advantages such as safety in numbers, and the combined strength and energy of the colony.

Many bugs gather in large numbers at certain times. They may want to court and mate, or they come together by chance, for example, to consume a rich food source, find shelter, or hibernate. They do not interact much, and they go their separate ways again.

Other insect species live together permanently in organized colonies. The only truly social insects are the hymenopterans – ants, bees, wasps – and the isopterans, or termites. As shown on the following pages, colony life is based around prolonged care of the young – a rare feature in the insect world.

"White ants"

Nicknamed "white ants," termites are a very ancient group of insects, related not to ants but to cockroaches. All termite species are colonial. Among the hymenopterans, all ants live in colonies and their high degree of organization closely resembles the termites. Bees and wasps show a range of lifestyles, from solitary to very social.

Setting up a colony

An insect colony is founded by one or more reproductive females, or queens. They have left the old nest, which may be too crowded, or damaged, or already occupied by other queens. These founders are sometimes accompanied by males, and sometimes by workers.

Left

When an ants' nest is broken open, their main concern is to get the larval cocoons to safety. Extra workers are summoned by danger pheromones, and the cocoons soon disappear from view.

• Among honeybees, workers follow the old queen when she leaves her nest to a young successor.

• Among tropical, stingless bees, it's a new, young queen that leads the swarm away.

• Young, winged, queen ants leave the colony on a mating flight, attended by males. Once mated, the queen chews off her wings and excavates a small nest for her first brood, which she feeds with her own saliva.

• Male and female termites excavate a suitable nest site together before they mate.

Right

Termite mounds have an air-conditioning and humidifying system that protects them from hot, dry climates. The air in the mound is heated by sun on its walls. The warm air rises up the central chimney, setting up a circulation that draws fresh air through the damp, subterranean galleries and up through the brood galleries into the fungus chambers.

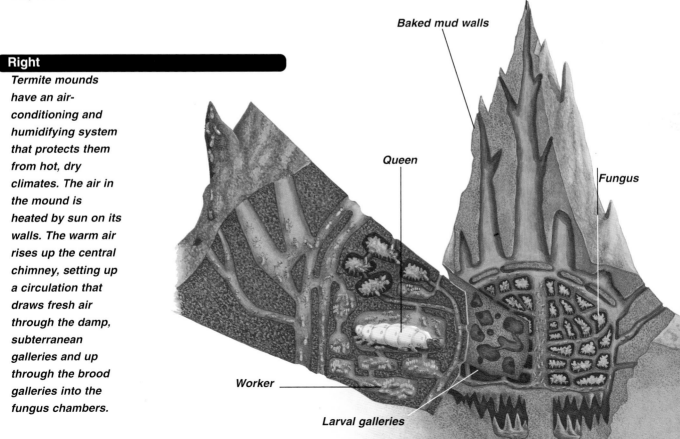

Central Chimney

Baked mud walls

Queen

Fungus

Worker

Larval galleries

Evolution of Social Life

Wasp and bee species show stages in the gradual evolution of a more and more complex social life.

Today, there is a range of bees and wasps with different degrees of social life. They show how the colonial lifestyle may have evolved through the ages.

The first important step was probably the provision of food for eggs laid in a nest. This occurs among many insects, including solitary wasps and bees. It represents a basic parent/offspring relationship, even though the parents then leave, so the two generations never see each other.

Overlapping lives

The next stage is for the lives of parent – invariably the mother – and offspring to overlap. Many female insects care for their young directly.

Above

Leafcutter ants feed themselves and their offspring on a special fungus or mold, which they grow in separate chambers within the nest. They cut pieces of leaf and carry them to the chamber for the fungus to grow on. Each ant species has its own species of fungus that grows nowhere else.

STAGE-BY-STAGE EVOLUTION OF BEE COLONIES

• *Solitary bees* Each female bee makes her own nest and provisions for her young. Examples: leafcutter bees, mining bees.
• *Shared nests* Sibling (sister) bees make cells in the same nest, but each provides food for her own young. Example: the mason bee *Osmia rufa*.
• *Quasi-social* This involves shared brood-rearing. Several sibling bees cooperate to build cells and feed the young in a communal nest. Example: the mason bee *Exomalopsis*.
• *Semi-social* There is division of labor. Some bees do not lay any eggs, but they help to feed the young of their siblings in the nest. Example: mining bees *Pseudaugochloropsis*.
• *Sub-social* Each female bee lives long enough to rear her brood to adulthood. This is part-way to overlapping generations. Example: the dwarf carpenter bee *Ceratina*.
• *Eu-social* Members of the first brood remain to help raise future broods. Example: the bumblebees *Bombus*.
• *Highly social* There are many specialized jobs done by several generations of highly organized nonbreeding individuals, the workers. Example: the honeybee *Apis mellifera*.

The beginnings of a social structure is shown by certain bees that build their single- or multicelled nests next to others of the same species. They are close neighbors.

Division of labor, or doing different jobs, is another phase. Individual bees take on specialized tasks, such as guarding the communal entrance to the nest, cleaning, or collecting food. They all still lay eggs, and their tasks benefit their own offspring as well as the offspring of the other bees.

Workers, not breeders

The next stage is for some bees to work, but not to breed. This may seem to contradict a basic law of nature, which is that each animal tries to pass its genes on to the next generation, so it cares for and protects only its own offspring. However, in social insects, all the colony members are related. The queen is the mother, and the workers are her daughters. Being one family, they all share genes. So, as the workers care for the next generations of eggs, larvae, and pupae, they are in effect caring for some of their own genes.

Would you believe?

People have been "stealing" honey from bees since the Stone Age. Cave paintings 9,000 years old show how honey was taken from bee nests high in trees. Then people realized that the bees would make more honey if some was removed and the nest was not totally destroyed. The next step was to encourage bees into specially arranged nest sites, such as hollow logs or upturned baskets.

Roof/lid

Air space

Sloping sides

Combs for honey or bee grubs

Entrance

Left

Modern bee-keeping is a precision science. Bee strains are carefully bred to be docile and to produce lots of honey. Partly made combs allow the bees to spend more time making honey. Farmers often move the hives nearer to fields of crops in flower so they can pollinate the flowers and improve the crop, yielding extra honey at the same time.

Jobs for the Workers

In the hustle and bustle of an insect colony, each individual must know its job and stick to it.

An individual insect has no choice in the role it plays within the colony. Its job is determined by its genes, its age, and the stage of the colony's development.

Castes

A group of individuals that perform one function in the insect colony is known as a caste. The reproductive caste consists of fertile males or kings and females or queens. They produce eggs and usually do little else. The nonreproductive castes are the workers, who build and maintain the nest, collect food, defend the colony, and care for the eggs, larvae, and pupae.

There are sometimes subcastes with different physical features, such as soldiers with large mandibles for biting enemies.

Communication

Communication among the members of an insect colony is mainly by touch, by scents called pheromones (see page 66), and by body chemicals known as hormones.

The pheromones are spread by touch, stroking, and mutual grooming. When two individuals meet, they groom each other and assess their pheromones. Any insect lacking the colony's distinctive odor is killed or driven out.

Hormones in control

Hormones are spread by trophallaxis, or food sharing. This occurs whenever individuals recognize each other. Each member of a caste secretes a hormone that prevents the young from developing into the same caste as itself. These hormones are passed around the colony during trophallaxis. When the level of one type of hormone drops, it allows development of new members for that particular caste. This ensures a balanced number of the different castes and subcastes in the nest.

Above

Many wasps build their nests from paper. They scrape wood from trees or fences, chew it, and mix it with saliva to form a pulp. Then they fashion this pulp into the cells of the small nest where the queen will lay her eggs.

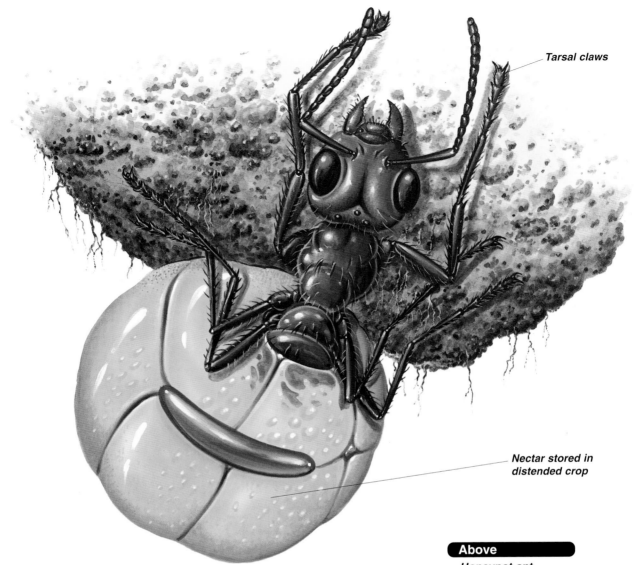

Tarsal claws

Nectar stored in distended crop

Honeypot ant repletes or "living larders" hang by their tarsal claws from the ceiling of their underground chamber. This specialized group of workers store sweet, high-energy honeydew inside their abdomens, so members of the colony can feed even when food outside is scarce.

TERMITES AND THEIR JOBS

In one termite colony, there may be several sizes of individuals who look as if they belong to different species. But they are all from the same species.

The **queen** is huge, with a swollen abdomen for egg laying.

The **king** is very large, and attends the queen.

The **workers** are "normal" size.

The **soldiers** have very big heads and large, strong mandibles.

Insect Architects

Insects are among the animal world's greatest builders, creating complex structures for shelter and protection.

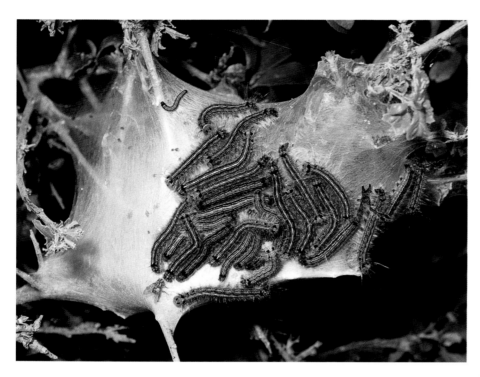

Above

These lackey-moth caterpillars have constructed a communal tent from hundreds of silk strands. They hide from enemies here when they are not feeding.

Insects rival spiders and birds as the best animal architects. Their jointed limbs and adaptable mouth parts can manipulate and process building materials with great precision. Bugs build homes as protection from extremes of climate, as defense against predators, and as places to rear their young and store food.

Camping out

Many caterpillars make "leaf tents" using the silk they produce from glands to stick the sides of leaves together. Others secrete themselves a solid cocoon before they change into pupae. This can incorporate bits such as leaf fragments or sand grains for disguise, or even the stinging bristles that the caterpillar sheds before pupation. Caddisfly larvae build themselves tube-shaped, camouflaged, mobile homes by sticking twigs, leaves, gravel, or sand to their silken tubes (see page 42).

Pots and combs

Ants, wasps, and bees construct a variety of homes for shelter and to raise their young. Some are simple burrows in the ground, wood, or even stone. Many wasps fashion pot nests from mud, often supported by plant fibers. Others, like the common wasp, use wood pulp (see page 102). Honeybees secrete the wax to mold their hexagonal combs inside a hollow tree, under a rocky overhang, or in a manmade beehive.

Left

The potter wasp skilfully constructs a tiny pot from mud mixed with its own saliva. She lays one egg in each pot, with a stung and paralyzed caterpillar as food, and seals the entrance.

Termite towerblocks

Tropical termites build the biggest constructions. Their mounds (see page 99) cased with dried, rock-hard mud, may be 2–3 yards (1.8–2.7m) high. They contain galleries, corridors and chambers to house the king and queen, eggs, larvae, pupae, and the fungus gardens that provide them with food. Much of the nest is underground, where the earth is cool and damp, even in a desert.

Would you believe?

Termites form the biggest groupings of social insects, by far. A single large, well-established termite mound may house more than five million termites of all castes – which is roughly equivalent to the numbers of humans in the big cities on earth. This compares with about 300,000 wood ants in a large ant-hill, around 50,000 bees in a man-made hive, and up to 2,000 wasps in a natural, fully-formed wasp nest.

Right

This African dung beetle is a master builder. It carefully rolls fresh dung into balls, which it will then bury and use to lay its eggs on. The balls also serve as protection from the fierce heat.

REPRODUCTION

INSECTS ARE VERY SUCCESSFUL AT REPRODUCING OTHER INSECTS, AND EMPLOY A HUGE VARIETY OF COURTSHIP BEHAVIORS AND DISPLAYS TO ATTRACT POTENTIAL MATES. ONCE THEIR PARTNER HAS BEEN SELECTED AND THE BUG COUPLE HAVE MATED, THE SEARCH FOR A SAFE PLACE FOR THE FEMALE TO LAY HER EGGS IS ON. HOWEVER, MOST BUGS DON'T MAKE GOOD PARENTS, AND INSTEAD LEAVE THEIR YOUNG TO FEND FOR THEMSELVES.

BUG EGGS HATCH INTO LARVAE, WHICH GROW THOUGH A PROCESS OF SHEDDING LAYERS OF SKIN UNTIL THEY ARE READY FOR THEIR GREAT TRANSITION — CALLED METAMORPHOSIS — IN WHICH THEY EXCHANGE THEIR LARVAL STATE FOR THE FULLY FLEDGED APPEARANCE OF THEIR ADULT FORM. IN BUTTERFLIES AND SOME OTHER GROUPS, THIS ALSO INCLUDES A PUPAL OR CHRYSALIS STAGE, WHICH IS THE "PRE-ADULT" STEP.

ONCE THE BUG REACHES ITS ADULTHOOD, THE CYCLE OF FEEDING, MATING, REPRODUCING, AND PERHAPS MIGRATING OR HIBERNATING IS REPEATED AGAIN UNTIL THE END OF ITS LIFE SPAN, WHEN IT IS REPLACED BY THE NEXT BUG GENERATION.

Making More Insects

The ultimate task of any insect is to produce offspring that will carry its genes to future generations.

Above

A female scorpion fly (left) feasts on the nuptial gift while the male mates with her. The feast will help to nourish the eggs she is about to lay.

Part of the insects' phenomenal success – in numbers of both species and individuals, and in their worldwide spread – is the way they reproduce. The vast majority of insects are oviparous, meaning they produce eggs, rather than giving birth to babies. And they lay huge numbers of eggs. The young that hatch out often live in a different habitat or place to the adults, thereby avoiding direct competition. The overall life cycle is short. These features allow insects to adapt to widely diverse environments, and also to cope with change.

The ultimate aim

In nature, reproduction is the "ultimate aim" for all living things. Enduring predators and bad conditions, and getting enough food and water, are the means to its end. What counts is to survive to sexual maturity, breed, and produce as many offspring as possible.

This not a conscious decision in the way that we might think about it. The powerful survival instincts of all creatures are driven by the need to pass on their genes to the next generation.

Some animals, like snails, are hermaphrodite, meaning male and female in the same individual. Insects are not. Every bug is either a male or a female.

Reproductive organs

The reproductive or sexual organs are in the abdomen. Males have two testes, composed of slender follicles, just above the intestine. These make the male sex cells or sperm. A sperm tube, the vas deferens, connects each testis to a sperm storage chamber, the seminal vesicle. These vesicles join to make one tube, the ejaculatory duct. This opens at the end of the male's outer or external sex organ, the penis.

Each female insect has a pair of ovaries, each composed of several tapering ovarioles. These make and store the female sex cells or eggs. The eggs are carried from the ovaries by egg ducts or oviducts, to the vagina. A seminal receptacle or sperm-receiving chamber is also connected to the vagina, which is then linked to the external sex organ, the ovipositor or egg-laying tube.

Insect sex

In most insects, the male and female court, then mate or copulate. The male introduces his sperm into the female's seminal receptacles. Then her eggs pass from the ovaries to the vagina. Here each is joined with, or fertilized by, a sperm. Then the fertilized eggs are laid.

Above

Damselflies adopt a mating-wheel posture for the transfer of sperm before the female (at bottom) lays her eggs.

Right

The reproductive organs of a female insect – here shown in a grotesque phasmid or leaf insect. The eggs are made in the ovaries, and their enveloping fluids and membranes are added as they pass along the oviduct.

Egg

Vagina

Oviducts

Spermatheca or seminal receptacles

Genital pore

Ovaries

Finding a Mate

Insects do not always accept the first mate to come along. There are the preliminaries of courtship.

In the world of bugs, courtship is not for fun. It ensures that an insect does not waste time and energy trying to mate with an individual from a different species, or one from the same species but of the same sex or not yet mature.

Types of courtship

Insects use sounds, sights, scents, pheromones, flashing lights, and many other means to attract potential mates from a distance (see pages 46–69). Generally, it is the male that does the attracting. Other insects get together by congregating at food or water sources, egg-laying sites, or genetically built-in landmarks. Still others are territorial – the male actively defends a place or resource that itself draws in females.

Above

The male dancefly catches a victim and giftwraps it in silky thread, to present to his prospective mate. If she accepts it (as here) he copulates with her as she is busy unwrapping and eating the present. But some males cheat – they wrap up bits of debris, or nothing at all. By the time the female discovers the bogus gift, the mating is done!

HOW TO ATTRACT A MATE

Insects have a huge variety of courtship behaviors and displays.
• Dragonfly males defend a territory suitable for the female to lay eggs.
• Damselfly males perform a "belly-flop" onto the water, to indicate a suitable egg-laying site for the female as she zigzags above.
• The male cockroach lifts his wings, exposing special glands on his back, and the female licks the secretions from these.
• Praying-mantis females give off a pheromone to attract males.
• Moth females attract males with pheromones.
• A cricket male "sings" to attract females, and the female then licks special secretions from his body.
• Stinkbug males release a pheromone that attracts females. The male then hits the female in the head to knock her over.
• Lacewings vibrate the twig on which they sit to attract a mate.
• Male tenebrionid beetles follow females across the desert sand, until eventually they become receptive or ready to mate.
• Some male scarab beetles clamp themselves on top of the female and stay there until she becomes receptive.

Scarab beetles

Contact courtship

Once the insects are in close contact, they indulge in mutual stroking, grooming, posturing, and special displays of flying or running. These activities ensure both male and female are from the same species, sexually mature, fit and healthy, primed, and ready to mate.

Choosing "Mr Right"

Throughout the animal kingdom, including the world of bugs, it is usually the males who try to attract the females – and then the female who chooses her male. She has much more to gain by choosing wisely. It takes more nutrients and energy to produce the eggs, compared to the tiny sperm. So the male courtship displays are designed to show how fit and suitable the male is as a mate. Then she selects the best male available, so that their offspring will be strong and healthy.

Above

Antlerfly males (Achias) perform a dance ritual to compare the lengths of their antlers or eye stalks. The male with the longest set wins and claims the attendant female.

Coming Together

During copulation or mating, the male passes his sperm cells into the female's body.

Many water creatures release their eggs or sperm from their bodies, so they float free. The sperm joins with or fertilizes an egg so it can begin its development. This is external fertilization. But in most land animals, including insects, fertilization is internal – inside the female's body. This prevents the eggs and sperm from drying out.

Locking genitals

In bugs, a mating pair join together their external sex organs or genitalia, so that sperm can pass from male to female. The male's genitalia are usually gripping structures, and the female's is the ovipositor or egg-laying tube. These are both modified appendages of the eighth and ninth abdominal segments.

Fertilization

The male everts or pushes out his penis during copulation. Muscle contractions force the sperm, in their fluid, along the ejaculatory duct and into the female's ovipositor. They then pass into the seminal receptacles or spermatheca, within the female's abdomen, for storage.

NO NEED FOR A MATE

Some female insects can reproduce without mating. Their eggs do not need fertilizing by sperm. This is called parthenogenesis. The males of the species may appear only at certain times of the year – or not at all, as the case may be.
• Aphids produce generation after generation of females without fertilization. Males do not appear until the autumn, when mating results in females laying tough eggs to survive the winter.

• In social bees, wasps, and ants, the unfertilized eggs develop into males, and the fertilized ones into females. All the workers in the colony are females. The only role of the males is to fertilize the queen.
• One type of calchid wasp lays her eggs inside the eggs of the silver Y moth. Each wasp's egg hatches into about 50 embryos. If the egg is fertilized, the embryos will be female. If not, they will be male.

• Likewise, gooseberry sawflies produce males from unfertilized eggs and females from fertilized ones.
• In the robin's pincushion gall-wasp, there is a very lopsided balance of the sexes, with only 1 male to 100 females.
• In the oakapple gall wasp, spring eggs hatch into females only. The summer brood produces both sexes.

The gap between mating and sperm transfer, and then egg-laying, varies from a few seconds to many months. Just before she lays her eggs, one sperm enters each egg through a microscopic opening, or micropyle, in its shell. The sperm and egg fuse at fertilization, and development of the egg into a young insect can begin.

Keeping away rivals

Each male insect tries to ensure that, after mating, the female has only his sperm for fertilization. This involves preventing other males from mating with her. Often, the male guards the female, keeping rivals at bay. In some species, male and female remain joined for long periods, before or after copulation. Or sometimes, the male inserts a blocking plug within the female's reproductive system.

Would you believe?

In a macabre mating ritual, the female praying mantis sometimes eats her mate head first, while copulation is in progress! But this is an important part of the mating act. Inside the male's head, a bundle of nerves restricts copulatory or mating movements. Once he is beheaded, his rear end can make the muscle actions and mating movements that pump sperm into her body.

Left

The male pond skater sits on the larger female, gripping her while he mates. Both of them float on the water's surface film, on their water-resistant, hairy feet.

When and Where to Lay

Female insects lay their eggs in safe places where the young have a ready source of food.

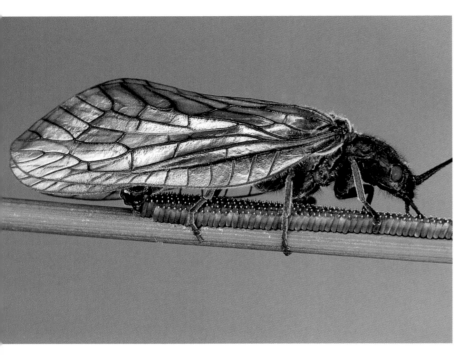

Above
The female alderfly lays her eggs carefully on a plant stem. She places them in a regular pattern and cements them in place with a special glue that she secretes.

Before they lay, most female insects require exact environmental conditions, such as temperature, light levels, and humidity. Often, they lay near the food source that their larvae will prefer. In some species, the ovipositor is very specialized for depositing the eggs at a specific site, such as cutting slits in plant stems, or boring holes in wood. Other species scatter eggs randomly, usually over water, and the nymphs are well able to look after themselves.

Egg variety

There are various egg-laying strategies. Those laid singly are easy to hide, but the constant movement and searching for sites taxes the female. Eggs laid in masses have the benefit of "safety in numbers." It is often possible to identify the type of insect from the way the eggs are grouped into clusters, rows, or other patterns, often cemented in place.

HOW MANY EGGS?

• The queen termite of the species *Belicositermes natalensis* lays 1,500 eggs each hour. This adds up to more than 10 million in a year – and she may live to 50 years! Her abdomen is swollen with eggs to a length of about 4 in. (10cm), so she cannot move at all. She depends on the rest of the colony for her every need.

• If all the offspring of a pair of houseflies survived, and continued to reproduce in turn, in four months they would cover the earth's surface to a depth of 16½ yds. (15m).

Size, shape, and surface

Egg size and shape also vary enormously. The smallest are invisible to the unaided human eye; the largest are about ¼in (6mm) long. Most are oval or spherical in shape, but some are like barrels, spindles, or even flowerpots. The colors range from plain white to bright hues like yellow and red.

Some eggs have ornate spines or ridges, others are smooth. To endure hostile conditions, such as desert heat or winter cold, many have tough, waterproof shells called chorions.

Left

The female giant ichneumon wasp lays her eggs into the larva or grub of a wood wasp while it is burrowing deep within dead wood. She feels for vibrations with her long antennae held against the bark. Then she drills into the wood with her 5 in. (13cm), stiletto-like ovipositor.

Would you believe?

A few insects do not lay eggs, but give birth to "babies" or live young. They include various kinds of aphids. There are two main methods. Oviparous females keep the eggs inside their bodies until they hatch, then give birth. Viviparous females retain and nourish the babies for a time after they have hatched, so they are born at a more advanced stage of development.

Left

The ovipositors of many wasps also work as stings that inject venom. Parasitic wasps use this venom to paralyze a "host," such as a caterpillar, on which their larvae will feed. Social wasps use the sting to defend the colony. Of these species, only the queen still has an ovipositor with an egg-laying function.

• A single cabbage aphid can give birth to young by parthenogenesis. If these offspring continued to reproduce, and had unlimited food and no predators, after one year they would weigh 740 million tons (755 million metric tonnes). That's more than three times the weight of every living person on earth!

Ovipositor used to sting victim

Insect Parents

Most insects do not care for their young, but some protect and nurture their offspring.

Some animals invest all their energies into producing huge numbers of eggs and offspring, in the hope that one or two will survive. They give little or no parental care. At the other end of the spectrum, there are creatures that have just a few offspring, but they spend time and energy caring for these, to give each one a better chance of survival. Most insects do the former, but a few do the latter.

Dangers to the eggs

Many insect eggs are eaten by predators, or attacked by parasitic insects, or infested with moldy fungi. The main job of an attentive bug-parent, usually the mother, is to protect the eggs from these dangers. The female earwig cleans her eggs of fungal spores, and like the mother mantis, defends them physically against parasites and predators.

Some insect mothers continue to protect the young after they have hatched. Certain tropical bug females stand on their heads and "buzz" the intruder. Some cockroaches lead their youngsters around in a line, while others carry them tucked under their wing cases.

Feeding

Most young insects can feed themselves as soon as they hatch, but a few rely on parental help. Some bug mothers shepherd the nymphs to better food sources, and help them to pierce the plant and suck the sap. Female earwigs vomit or regurgitate food for their hatchlings. Some female cockroaches even produce a special milk-like secretion that the young lap. Also, certain crickets and ants produce nonfertile eggs for the young to eat.

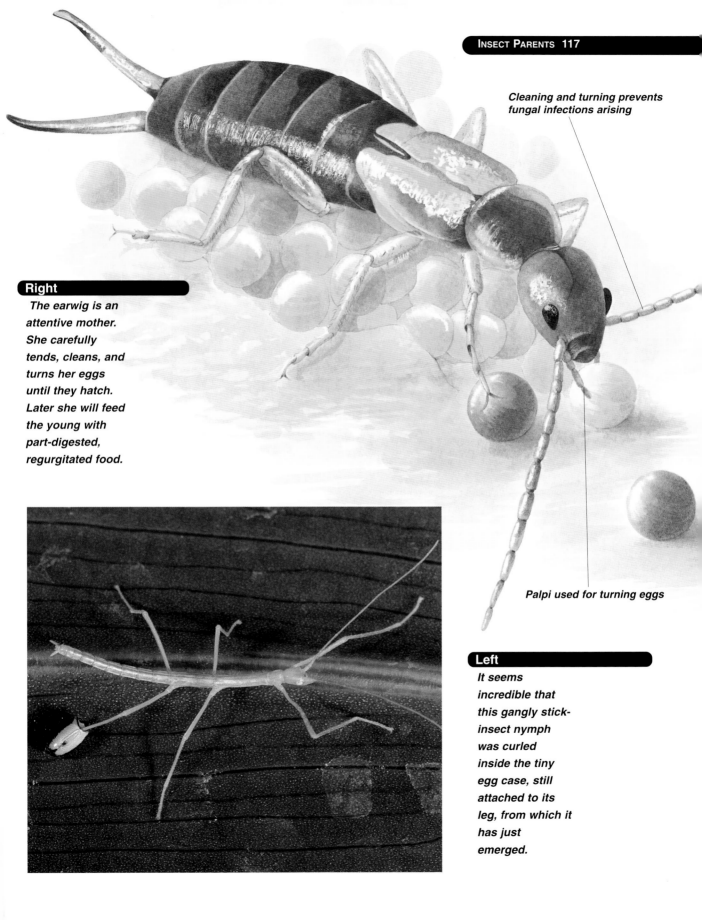

Cleaning and turning prevents
fungal infections arising

Right

The earwig is an
attentive mother.
She carefully
tends, cleans, and
turns her eggs
until they hatch.
Later she will feed
the young with
part-digested,
regurgitated food.

Palpi used for turning eggs

Left

It seems
incredible that
this gangly stick-
insect nymph
was curled
inside the tiny
egg case, still
attached to its
leg, from which it
has just
emerged.

Eating Machines

A larva's job is to eat and grow, accumulating enough nourishment to reach adulthood – and perhaps survive this, too.

Insect eggs hatch into the next stage of the life cycle, the larvae. These are "eating machines" that grow very rapidly by molting or shedding skin. Some larvae resemble their parents, while others look very different (see pages 122–123).

A confusion of names

There are many common and confusing names for the various types of insect larvae. In beetles, wasps, and bees, they are called grubs. In flies, they are known as maggots. Butterfly and moth larvae are known as caterpillars, while some are called worms. Grasshoppers, crickets, and locusts are termed nymphs. Dragonflies, damselflies, and others with aquatic larvae are called naiads.

Above

The ladybug larva is an active hunter. Like its parent, its favorite food is aphids. It is protected by its poisonous, spiny hairs, which break off if the larva is molested.

HOW FAST DO THEY GROW?

• The caterpillar of a polyphemus moth *(Antheraea polyphemus)* increases its weight by approximately 4,000 times in its 56 days as a larva. At the same rate, a normal-sized, human newborn baby would grow to 13 tons (11,800kg)!
• A honeybee grub, fed on nutritious pollen, increases its weight by 1,500 times in 5 days.
• The goat-moth caterpillar, fed on wood, increases in weight by 72,000 times in 3 years.
• Fleshfly maggots, feasting on rotting flesh, increase their weight by 450 times in 3 days.

• The great water beetle larva, catching pond creatures like tadpoles, increases in weight 50 times in as many days.
• "Silkworms" are silk-moth caterpillars. On silk farms they are kept in carefully controlled conditions and fed every few hours on fresh mulberry leaves. They grow in weight by 70 times in 5 weeks, to a length of about 3 in. (8cm) before spinning their silken cocoons.

Silkworm

Larval types

There are four official scientific types of insect larvae:

• Campodeiform larvae are named after a primitive group of wingless insects, which they resemble. They have three pairs of well-developed, jointed, thoracic legs, and no other legs. Most insect groups, from fleas and cockroaches to grasshoppers and lacewings, have larvae of this type.

• Scarabaeiform larvae are named after the young of scarab beetles. They have less well-developed thoracic legs and a large, fleshy, C-shaped abdomen. They usually live in loose soil or forest debris. The grubs of stag and cockchafer beetles belong to this type.

• Eruciform larvae have long, slim bodies, jointed thoracic legs, and abdominal false legs or prolegs. They include moth and butterfly caterpillars and sawfly larvae.

• Vermiform (worm-like) larvae have no legs at all. Fly maggots and the grubs of bees, wasps, and ants are in this group. Some can wriggle like worms; others are almost immobile.

Would you believe?

 The American periodic cicada spends 17 years as a larva, buried underground, sucking sap from plant roots. Its egg is laid in a plant stem, then when the tiny nymph hatches, it falls to the ground and tunnels with its spade-like front legs. Development takes a long time because the food is not very nutritious. Finally, the nymph climbs up a tree trunk, and then sheds its skin for the last time.

Left

"Mealworms," which infest some food stores, are the larvae of darkling beetles. They are bred as food for carnivorous pets such as birds and snakes, and are reared on nothing more than bran.

Shedding Skin

The insect's hard body-casing has a drawback – it restricts growth. The answer is to shed it and grow a new one.

Insect skin shedding or molting is known as ecdysis, and it is under the control of hormones (see page 102). It happens several times during the larval stage, according to the species.

Through the breach

The old exoskeleton, known as the exuvium, is loosened from the underlying epidermis by a special molting fluid. This breaks down the inner layer of the old cuticle, weakening it sufficiently to be ruptured by the expanding body within. The split is usually along the back of the thorax. The now-soft and pale larva pulls itself through the breach and grows very rapidly, before the new cuticle dries and hardens.

The period between molts, when there is very little growth, is called a stadium. The insect itself at this time is known as a larval stage, or instar.

Numbers and variations

Most insects undergo from 4 to 12 molts between hatching from the egg and turning into an adult. A few have up to 40 molts. The number may vary according to the conditions and amounts of food, even within the same species.

Above

After molting, a swallowtail caterpillar eats its old skin. This is common among insect larvae, since they recycle important nutrients.

HOW MANY MOLTS?

These are typical numbers of molts in the whole life cycle.

Stonefly

Flies	2 times
Grasshoppers	5 times
Cockroaches	7 times
Moths and butterflies	5-9 times
Mayflies and stoneflies	30-40 times

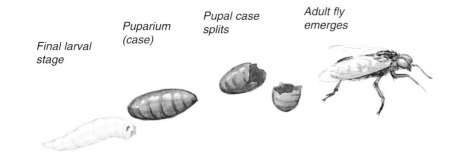

Final larval
stage

Puparium
(case)

Pupal case
splits

Adult fly
emerges

How an insect larva molts

First, the larva finds a damp, secluded place and hangs upside down.
The old cuticle is then separated from the new one by a secretion called
molting fluid. The larva puffs itself up with air, and the old skin splits along
a line across the back of the thorax. This provides an escape hole for the
larva, which wriggles free of the old skin. The larva stays in its hiding
place, avoiding dryness and predators, while its cuticle gradually hardens
and takes on the required colors. Meanwhile, it grows rapidly.

Except for a few primitive wingless insects, molting and growth stop
when the insect reaches its adult stage.

Would you believe?

Molting is controlled
by a hormone
produced in a special gland
in the insect's head. The
hormone, ecdysin, is carried
around the body in the
blood, until it reaches the
epidermis. Here the molting
glands release molting fluid
beneath the old cuticle, and
the epidermal cells begin to
secrete the new cuticle.

The Great Change

Most young insects look different from their parents.
The change to adult form is called metamorphosis.

Molting not only allows an insect to grow. It also allows the immature and adult stages to have different body forms and so live different lifestyles. Most young insects specialize in feeding and growing. Adults, on the other hand, concentrate their efforts on reproduction. The change in body shape and form along the way is known as metamorphosis.

None at all

Some wingless insects, including silverfish and firebrats, show almost no metamorphosis. When they hatch from their eggs, they already look almost exactly like their parents. They change little, except in size, as they molt and grow. This is called ametabolous development.

Above

Stag beetle larvae are plump and white, and live in old wood. They change into the pupal form shown on page 124.

YOUNG AND ADULT

This chart compares the young and adult forms of two insects, showing incomplete and complete metamorphosis.

Grasshopper – incomplete metamorphosis

Nymph	*Adult*
chewing mouth parts	chewing mouth parts
compound eyes	compound eyes
shorter antennae	longer antennae
wing buds	fully formed wings
long legs	long legs

Butterfly – complete metamorphosis

Caterpillar	*Adult*
chewing mouth parts	sucking mouth parts
simple eyes	compound eyes
very short antennae	long antennae
no wing buds	wings
short legs	long legs

Not complete

In other insects, the very young forms look vaguely like their parents – and they resemble them more and more with each molt. These types of larvae are known as nymphs, or if they live in the water, naiads.

Towards the last molts, the nymph's wings develop as external pads or wing buds. Finally, the last nymph stage or instar molts directly to the adult form. This is called hemimetabolous development, or incomplete metamorphosis. It is found among grasshoppers, crickets, cockroaches, fleas, lice, stoneflies, mayflies, dragonflies, damselflies, true bugs, and similar groups.

Complete

Complete metamorphosis or holometabolous development is more dramatic. The larva passes through a resting stage, called the pupa, before it reaches adulthood. The wings develop as internal sacs beneath the larva's skin, and turn inside out during the pupal stage. Insects which have complete metamorphosis are butterflies and moths, true flies, beetles, bees, wasps, and ants.

Would you believe?

Some larvae eat so much that, when they become adults, they need no food. These include mayflies, nonbiting midges, and emperor moths. The adults only live long enough to reproduce, and they may have no mouth parts. On the other hand, some species do not feed at all as larvae. Certain blood-sucking fly females give their offspring such a nutritious start in life that these can survive until they themselves become blood-sucking adults.

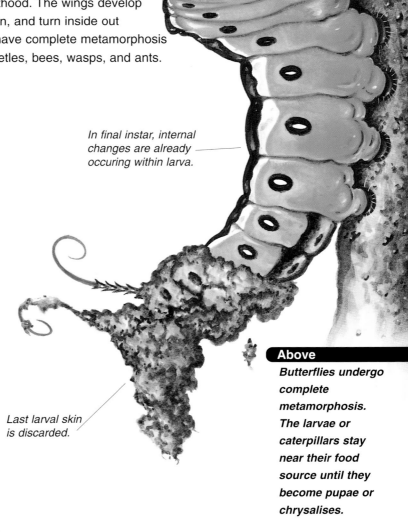

Adult mouth parts will be quite different to larval mouth parts.

In final instar, internal changes are already occuring within larva.

Last larval skin is discarded.

Above

Butterflies undergo complete metamorphosis. The larvae or caterpillars stay near their food source until they become pupae or chrysalises.

Not at Rest

**The pupa looks like a resting stage between larva and adult.
But inside, dramatic changes are taking place.**

Insects that undergo complete metamorphosis have a next-to-last stage in the life cycle, called the pupa. A butterfly or moth pupa is commonly known as a chrysalis.

The pupa is usually hard-cased, legless and wingless. It seems completely inactive. Yet inside, most of the larval tissues are broken down and reassembled into the adult organs, legs, wings, and other parts. The reassembly takes place around small, simple, growth buds that the larva has, but that do not develop. In fact the transformation begins as the larva becomes inactive during its final instar, before it pupates, when its final molt exposes the pupa.

Above

After three years of feeding, the fat stag-beetle larva curls up in readiness to become a pupa.

Pupal protection

Most fly maggots form cylindrical pupae inside their last larval skins, which are now called puparia. The puparium forms a protective layer. Other larvae spin a protective silk cocoon, or silken girdles, guyropes, and pads to hang from when they become pupae. The larva may incorporate bits of the surroundings into the cocoon, for camouflage.

CHRYSALISES AND COCOONS

• The skipper butterfly makes a loose silk cocoon, incorporating bits of grass and leaves as disguise for the pupa or chrysalis within.
• The swallowtail butterfly produces a chrysalis attached to a plant stem, by a silk pad at the bottom and a girdle halfway up. The chrysalis is the same color as its twig.
• The tortoiseshell butterfly chrysalis hangs from its silk pad.
• Hawkmoth caterpillars pupate in a loose chamber in the soil.

• The puss-moth caterpillar makes a silk cocoon incorporating bark shavings, which disguise it against the tree trunk.
• A stag beetle larva pupates in a chamber in rotten wood.
• Ant larvae make silk cocoons as they become pupae. These are sold as "ants' eggs" for aquarium fish. The workers cut open the cocoons so the new adults can emerge.
• The alderfly nymph makes a mud chamber in which to pupate.

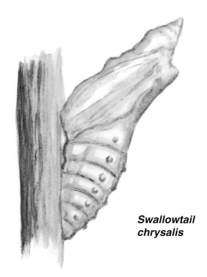

Swallowtail chrysalis

Emergence

The final emergence of the adult from the pupal case is called eclosion –
and it is one of nature's most amazing sights. It is triggered by factors
such as light, temperature, air pressure, humidity, or some combination
of these.

Adults escape their pupal cases in various ways. Some have chewing
mouth parts. Others have special cutters on their legs, or pressure
organs that they can inflate, or secretions that dissolve the pupal case.

Above

*This common
morpho butterfly
has just emerged
from its pupal
case. Its wings are
still crumpled and
its body soft.*

The Final Stage

The last stage in the insect's life is the adult – then the whole cycle starts again.

A new adult insect, just emerged from its last molt, is soft, flexible, pale, and wet, with crumpled wings. It is helpless and vulnerable until its exoskeleton has hardened. It must also clean itself of pupal or nymphal case fragments, molting fluid, and the body wastes called meconium that accumulated during the pupal stage. Insects with complicated mouth parts or ovipositors have to fit the separate sections together. Only when all this is complete can the insect set out to find food or a mate.

Right

The miracle-like transformation of a waterbound dragonfly nymph into a superb aerial hunter takes only hours. The nymph climbs up a reed stem early on a sunny summer morning. The cuticle behind its head splits, and the adult dragonfly emerges.

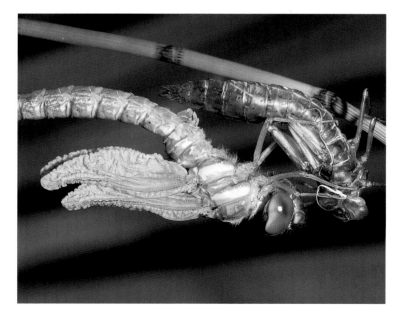

Ready to mate

Most adult insects are ready to mate very soon after they emerge, even though the females may not lay their eggs for some time afterwards. Once copulation has occurred, the male's main role is finished. In some species, he stays with his mate to guard her, or he might mate again. Usually, however, his life is over. Most females survive only until the eggs are fully developed, and laid in a suitable place. Then they too succumb to predators, injury, or disease.

Above

The adult stag beetle at last emerges from its pupal case

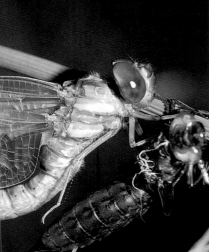

Below

A cicada nymph has spent many years underground, sucking sap from plant roots. At some unknown signal, it crawls up a tree trunk and clings to the bark with its claws. The larval skin splits, and the crumpled adult pulls itself free.

The life cycle of the swallowtail butterfly begins when the female – after mating – lays her eggs on milk parsley, the food plant of the caterpillar is transformed into another beautiful butterfly via the pupal or chrysalis stage.

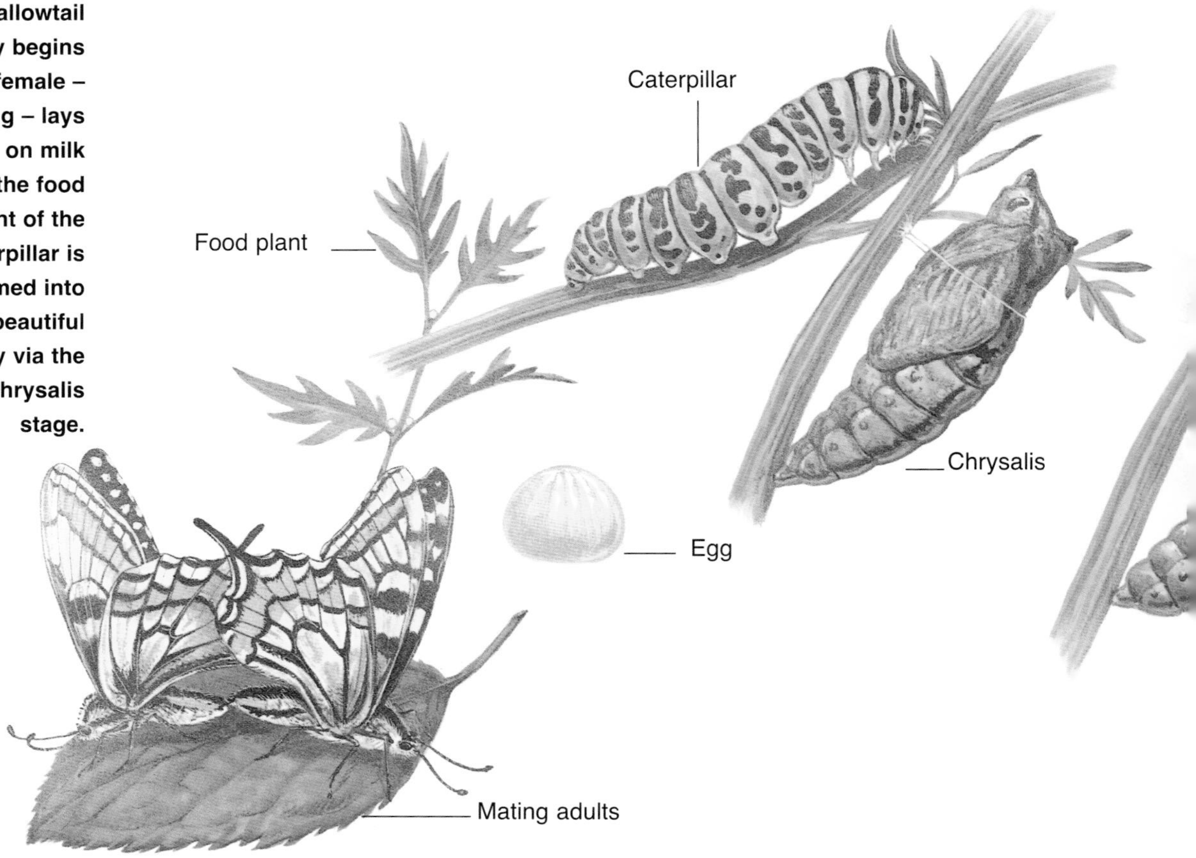

Caterpillar

Food plant

Chrysalis

Egg

Mating adults

HOW LONG DO THEY LIVE?

These are average time spans for various insects in the different phases of their life cycles.
(Short time is usually a few days, but variable)

	Larva	Pupa	Adult
Dragonfly	More than 2 years	None	Less than 4 months
Assassin bug	2 months	None	3 months
Ant lion	More than 3 years	1 month	2 months
Burnet moth	About 4 years	Short time	3 weeks
Blowfly	1 week	1 week	2 weeks
Diving beetle	9 months	Short time	3 years
Minotaur beetle	3 months	3-4 weeks	Hibernation
Stag beetle	3 years	Hibernation	1 month
Ladybug	3 weeks	Short time	Hibernation

Adult emerges

Would you believe?

Mayflies belong to the group Ephemeroptera, which means "winged insects that live but a day." The adult's life span is only a few hours. At dusk, swarms of them emerge by molting from a specialized, flying, last-nymph stage called the sub-adult. They are the only insects to have this "extra" phase in the life cycle. They mate in a frenzied nuptial flight, and the females immediately drop their eggs into the water. In some species, the female dives deep into the water to lay her eggs, and drowns. They are all dead before dawn!

The yearly cycle

In temperate regions, most insect life cycles last for only one year and fit within the seasons. There is usually just one generation per year. This means that at any time of year, there is only one stage of the life cycle present. Most spend the winter in a dormant state, as eggs, larvae, nymphs, pupae, or even adults. But if the conditions and weather are favorable, the first adults may be able to breed and produce a second generation. This can lead to serious pest outbreaks when their numbers multiply.

In tropical regions, insect life cycles are linked to changing conditions of the wet and dry seasons.

Insect Ecology

INSECTS HAVE A CRUCIAL ROLE IN THE ECOLOGY OF ALMOST ALL THE WORLD'S HABITATS. THEY ARE VERY CLOSELY CONNECTED WITH FLOWERS THROUGH POLLINATION, IN WHICH THE INSECTS ACT AS TRANSPORTERS OF POLLEN (MALE SEX CELLS) FROM ONE FLOWER TO ANOTHER OF ITS KIND, SO THAT THE PLANTS ARE ABLE TO REPRODUCE. **I**N RETURN FOR THE INSECTS' ROLE IN AIDING PLANT REPRODUCTION, PLANTS FEED INSECTS THROUGH THEIR NECTAR, SO THEY HAVE A HELPFUL, TWO-WAY RELATIONSHIP.

ALTHOUGH INSECTS CAN BE DESTRUCTIVE PESTS, AND ARE OFTEN CARRIERS OF DISEASES THAT ARE EXTREMELY HARMFUL TO CROPS, LIVESTOCK, AND HUMANS, MANY OF THEM ARE ALSO HIGHLY USEFUL. FOR EXAMPLE, BURROWING INSECTS KEEP THE SOIL HEALTHY FOR FARMING; BEES PRODUCE HONEY; SOME BUGS PRODUCE DYES AND OTHER SUBSTANCES; AND CERTAIN BUGS, SUCH AS GRUBS, ARE VALUED BY SOME PEOPLE AS FOOD BECAUSE THEY ARE EDIBLE AND PACKED WITH PROTEIN. **S**OME ARE EVEN CONSIDERED A DELICACY!

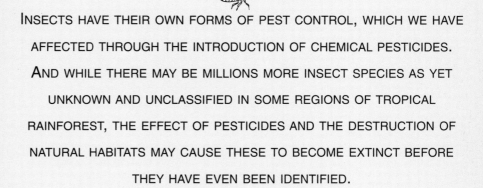

INSECTS HAVE THEIR OWN FORMS OF PEST CONTROL, WHICH WE HAVE AFFECTED THROUGH THE INTRODUCTION OF CHEMICAL PESTICIDES. **A**ND WHILE THERE MAY BE MILLIONS MORE INSECT SPECIES AS YET UNKNOWN AND UNCLASSIFIED IN SOME REGIONS OF TROPICAL RAINFOREST, THE EFFECT OF PESTICIDES AND THE DESTRUCTION OF NATURAL HABITATS MAY CAUSE THESE TO BECOME EXTINCT BEFORE THEY HAVE EVEN BEEN IDENTIFIED.

Insect Ecology

Without insects, we'd be knee-deep in animal dung, and have no flowers to brighten our world!

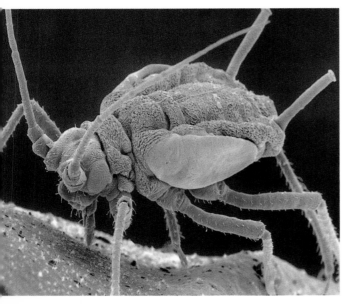

Above

An aphid (magnified 90 times) sucks sap from the stem of a rose. A large infestation of aphids stops the sap flowing to the leaves above.

Ecology is the study of how plants and animals live together and relate to each other in their surroundings. An ecological niche is an organism's "place" in nature. The niche is like the role or job of a living thing. It is defined by many factors, such as temperature, requirements for food and shelter, interactions with competitors and rivals, and effects on other species.

Small insects, small niches

Insects are generally small, so they can occupy niches too small or specialized for larger animals like birds and mammals. In their mini-world, insects generally avoid direct, day-to-day competition and conflict with these bigger creatures.

Eaten and eating

Because insects are so abundant, many animals – even some plants – have evolved as insectivores to eat them. Insects are probably the third most-significant food source in the world, after trees, grasses, and similar plants, and the plankton in seas and lakes.

Scale insects suck the sap from plant stems, which interferes with the circulation of nutrients within the plant, and may also introduce disease.

Many insect larvae tunnel through leaves as they feed. This reduces the leaves' efficiency and causes the entire plant to suffer.

The vast numbers of insects must eat, too. Some are plant-eaters or herbivores, consuming almost every part of every plant. Despite our perceptions, relatively few species prefer our farm crops, but sometimes they occur in huge numbers. Other insects are hunters or predators, especially of their fellow insects. Some are parasites, usually on larger animals.

Rotting insects

Perhaps the most valuable, but unsung, role of insects is to scavenge and decompose. Life could not continue without the constant recycling of the earth's resources, especially the dead bodies of animals and plants, and animal droppings. Scavenging insects are at the front line. They chew up these "wastes" and pass them on, as their own feces, to more rotters such as bacteria and fungi. The bacteria and fungi break them down further to basic nutrients that plants can use, so completing the cycle.

Above

The hummingbird clearwing moth hovers to drink nectar from the nectaries deep inside a flower. It unrolls its long, tube-like proboscis and sucks up the sweet, high-energy liquid.

Insects and Flowers

Flowering plants and insects evolved together, each causing and responding to changes in the other.

Above

A hairy hummingbird hawk moth becomes covered with pollen as it delves for nectar amongst the petals of a fuschia flower. It will transfer the pollen to other flowers on its nocturnal rounds.

Perhaps the most intimate of ecological relationships is between flowering plants and their insect pollinators. Pollination is the transfer of plant pollen – microscopic grains like yellowish dust, containing male sex cells – from one flower to another of the same kind. This allows the male cells to join or fertilize the female sex cells, or eggs, in the flower. These then grow into seeds.

Wind and insects

There are two main methods of pollination – wind and insects. Wind-pollinated flowers produce very light pollen grains that drift in the air. But it's a hit-and-miss process. The flowers have to make and release so many millions of pollen grains that some hit the mark only by chance.

Insect-pollinated plants depend entirely on their six-legged beneficiaries to visit their flowers, collect the pollen grains by a multitude of means from the male parts, and deliver them to the female parts of another flower in the same species. Some flowers are adapted to relatively chance pollination by any type of passing insect, or even another animal like a mouse or spider. Others have evolved very specific relationships, sometimes with just a single insect species.

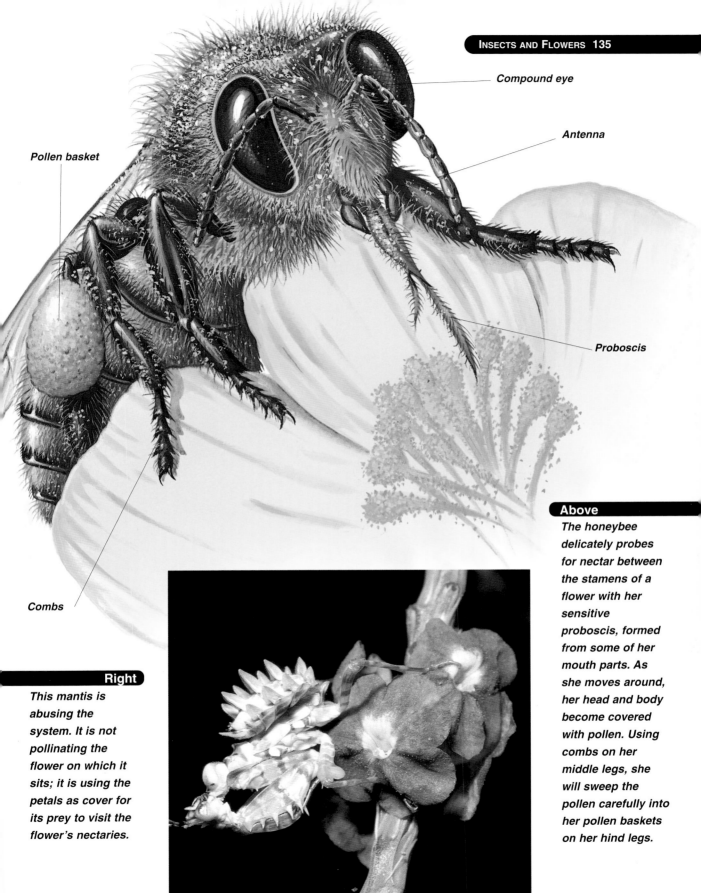

Compound eye

Antenna

Pollen basket

Proboscis

Combs

Above

The honeybee delicately probes for nectar between the stamens of a flower with her sensitive proboscis, formed from some of her mouth parts. As she moves around, her head and body become covered with pollen. Using combs on her middle legs, she will sweep the pollen carefully into her pollen baskets on her hind legs.

Right

This mantis is abusing the system. It is not pollinating the flower on which it sits; it is using the petals as cover for its prey to visit the flower's nectaries.

Hand in hand

The insect-flower relationship goes way back. Plants with simple flowers first appeared in the Cretaceous period, about 130 million years ago, during the time of the dinosaurs. They were probably pollinated by beetles and flies that fed on the pollen as well as transferring some of it.

About 100 million years ago, fossils show a simultaneous burgeoning of plant and insect species. Flowers began to color the landscape as they developed more and more sophisticated ways to attract their insect partners, as described on the following pages.

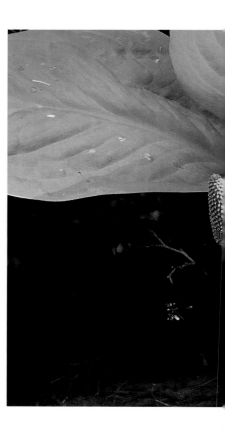

Right

Flies, attracted by the smell of decay, become trapped at the base of this cuckoo-pint arum lily's central spike. They pollinate the tiny flowers during their struggle to escape.

POLLINATION – INSECT OR WIND?

• **Wind-pollinated plants** produce enormous quantities of light pollen grains that float about on air currents. It's pure chance if the grains land on another flower of the correct species. Typical wind-pollinated flowers are small, with inconspicuous petals and no scent, since these are not needed to attract insects. Instead, they have protruding stamens (male parts) that release large amounts of pollen, and elaborate feathery carpels (female parts) to catch them.

• **Insect-pollinated flowers** often have large, showy, colorful petals to attract insects by color. They also give off strong scents to attract insects by smell, and nectar to reward them with a sweet meal. The flower is intricately shaped to allow the insects in, and the stamens are positioned to brush their pollen against it. Likewise, the carpels are placed to rub insects that have already gathered pollen.

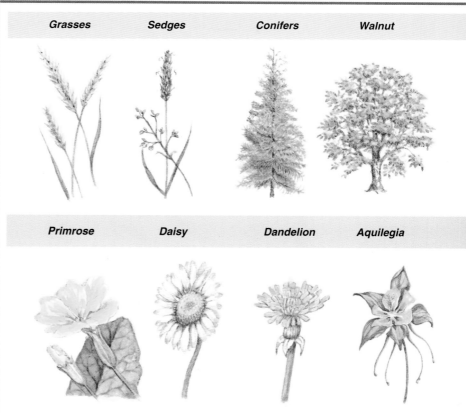

Grasses   Sedges   Conifers   Walnut

Primrose   Daisy   Dandelion   Aquilegia

Would you believe?

• The yucca plant and yucca moth cannot live without each other. The flower's stamens (male parts) are shaped so that only the specialized mouth parts of the female moth can gather the pollen. She forms the grains into a ball, which she carefully pushes into the carpel (female part) of another yucca flower, as she lays her egg there too. The egg hatches into a caterpillar that eats some of the pollen and developing seeds – but not all. The two species are entirely dependent on each other, and are an example of what ecologists call "obligate symbiosis."

Oak	Birch	Poplar	Hazel

Iris	Snapdragon	Angelica	Evening primrose	Comfrey	Foxglove

How Flowers Attract Insects

Flowers and their insect pollinators are nature's ultimate examples of cooperation.

Flowers do not have brightly colored petals and beautiful fragrances simply for our appreciation. These features have evolved to attract pollinating insects, although people have selected and bred some blooms to enhance the hues and scents.

Colors

Insect eyes (see page 48) are very sensitive to colors toward the ultraviolet end of the light spectrum. This is why many flower petals are purple, blue, or violet. Flowers that bloom at night are usually white or pale yellow, and are highly scented to attract nocturnal insects.

Scents

Many flower scents are sweet or sugary, to advertise their nectar. But not all flowers are so sweet. Purple trilliums (*Trillium erectum*) and skunk cabbage (*Symplocarpus foetidus*) smell like decaying meat in order to lure their particular pollinators – flesh flies – who like to lay their eggs in rotting animal carcasses.

Above

The snapdragon flower normally stays tightly shut, protecting its nectaries from small insects. Only the bumblebee is heavy enough to open the complicated mechanism and crawl inside. As it does so, it gets covered in pollen.

FLOWERS AND THEIR POLLINATORS

Can you work out how these flowers are adapted to their insect pollinators?

Cow parsleys and general insects, such as flies, beetles, ants, and bees

Nectar

Plant nectar or "honey" is a syrupy fluid packed with high-energy sugars. It is a valuable food source for many insects, especially butterflies, and lures them to the flowers. Many petals have honey guidelines that lead the insect in toward the nectaries at the flower's base. Some honey guidelines are visible to us, but others only show up at the ultraviolet end of the light spectrum. We can't see them, but insects can.

Left

A bumblebee in search of nectar follows the honey guidelines that appear as dark lines or shapes on the petals of a mallow flower.

Shape

The general shape of a flower gives clues to the identity of the pollinators. Deep trumpet or tubular blooms force the insect to push bodily down into the flower, rubbing against the male and female parts in the process.

The length of an insect's proboscis (tubular mouth parts, see page 74) is important. For example, many insects can reach the nectaries of white clover (*Trifolium repens*). But only bumblebees have a proboscis long enough to penetrate the long flower of red clover (*Trifolium pratense*).

Hairy or smooth?

There are many other aspects to flower-insect partnerships. Hairy-bodied insects like bees and bumblebees carry more pollen than smooth insects such as beetles and ants. Also, insect-dependent flowers usually open only during the peak activity period of the species they seek to attract. So, moth-pollinated flowers spread their petals at night, and butterfly-pollinated ones by day.

Would you believe?

• Some flowers that invite pollinating insects to visit them are really death traps. There may be a crab spider lurking within, colored to match the petals. Or the whole flower may really be a flower mantis, ready to kill and consume the unwary visitor.
• Some tropical orchids have an amazing resemblance to female bees. The male bees of the species try to mate with them, but instead they collect pollen. This is an example of mimicry.

Orchids and hawkmoths

Tropical aquilegia and the hummingbird moths

Figs and fig wasps

Rafflesia and carrion flies

Galling Insects

Plants have various defenses against insects who try to eat them.

Tough bark and leaves, stinging hairs, thorns, repulsive odors, distasteful substances and even poisons – these are just a few of the defenses that plants have evolved against insects. Some plants also protect themselves from an irritation or physical injury, like an animal scratch or bite, by producing a gall.

A gall is a growth or proliferation of tough plant tissue that seals off and protects the damaged area. It's rather like a cut in our own skin, which clots and scabs, and then heals over with tough scar tissue.

Above

There are some 60 different chambers inside this robin's-pincushion gall, each containing a tiny wasp grub.

The gall makers

The gall formers or gall makers are insects who take advantage of this type of plant defense. The largest group of gall makers are certain flies, especially gall midges, followed by gall wasps, gall weevils, some long-horned beetles, metallic woodborers, gall aphids, some species of micromoths, and the tiny, midge-like group called Thysanoptera or thrips.

TYPES OF GALLS

The insects that make plant galls are best identified by the shape of their galls. The tiny wasps are very hard to tell apart, but their galls are very distinctive. No one really knows why different insects can cause the same plant to produce such a variety of growths.

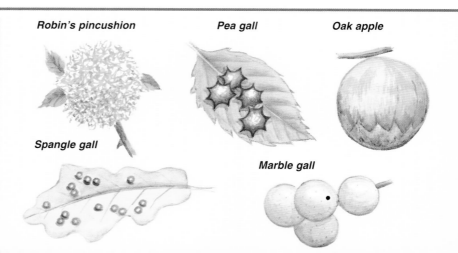

Robin's pincushion

Pea gall

Oak apple

Spangle gall

Marble gall

Left

Another gall of oak, the woolly oak gall, is caused by a tiny, reddish-brown wasp with yellow legs. The galls form on male catkins.

Inside the gall

The process begins when the adult insect lays an egg in the plant tissue. The plant produces the gall swelling in response to the presence of the egg, or to chemical secretions given off by the larva when it hatches. These secretions mimic plant hormones called auxins that normally stimulate and regulate the plant's growth.

As the larva grows inside its gall container, the plant provides it with shelter from the weather, protection from predators, and all the food it can eat! Eventually, the last-stage larva or adult insect exits, often by chewing a small hole through to the outside.

Types of galls

The gall's size, shape, and color are highly characteristic of the insect species inside. The largest are bigger than golf balls; the smallest are almost microscopic. They may be perfect spheres or other geometric shapes, or irregular masses. Many have interesting names like oak-apple galls, spangle galls, turban galls, and robin's-pincushion galls. Galls may look unsightly, but they are usually no more than a minor nuisance for the host plant.

Would you believe?

Italian biologist-physician Marcello Malpighi discovered the true nature of tiny galls in the mid 1600s. He studied the development and contents of the swellings with the newly invented microscope. Until this time, people had seen adult gall wasps appearing from plant galls, and believed them to be examples of "spontaneous generation" or life created from nonliving matter.

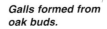

Right

Marble galls formed from the buds on an oak twig. The hole is where a tiny wasp has chewed its way through.

Galls formed from oak buds.

Hole indicates a wasp has chewed its way through.

Insects of Value

Insects are often perceived as pests and disease carriers, but many are our allies.

Insects are inextricably woven into the web of life. Sometimes they have adverse effects on ourselves. But we also have much to thank them for. For example, billions of tiny, burrowing insects loosen the soil, make tunnels to aerate it, recycle the soil nutrients, and generally keep the earth healthy and fertile.

Helping the farmer

Some herbivorous insects feed on noxious weeds, helping to control them. And some predatory insects eat other insects that are plant pests, thereby helping the farmer. The value of insect predators, such as ladybug beetles, mantids and lacewings, is often undervalued, and many more species might be pressed into this service of biological control (see page 144).

Above

People in ancient China discovered how to make silk from the fine threads of silkworm cocoons. These are not true worms, but the larvae or caterpillars of the silk moth Bombyx mori. They spin the silken cocoons around them as they turn into pupae.

Many uses

Perhaps the world's premier insect pollinators are honeybees. They are kept all over the world on farms, fields, orchards, and flower nurseries, where they produce honey and beeswax, in addition to their vital pollen-distributing role.

Insect cuisine

Insects even supply people with nutritious meals. Native Australians eat "witchetty grubs," the various larvae of beetles and moths, and honeypot ants. In Asia, grasshoppers and locusts are often on the menu. In different parts of Africa, people cook locusts, grasshoppers, beetles, ant pupae, honeyants, and even mosquitoes baked into pies.

Certain sap-sucking bugs exude a type of honeydew, or manna. It can be used as a sweetener for our food or fermented into a type of alcoholic drink. Many pampered goldfish thrive on "ant's eggs," which are really dried ant pupae.

Would you believe?

• The silk produced by a cultivated silkworm caterpillar is one thousandth of an inch (0.025mm) thick and 5000 ft. (1500m) long.
• Each silkworm can produce 700 eggs.
• The silk produced by wild silkworms, called "tussah silk," is brown and hairy, and is three times thicker than that of cultivated silkworms.
• Sericulture, or silkworm farming, originated in China 500 years ago.

Left

For thousands of years, people have taken advantage of the honeybee (see page 135), and not only for their nutritious honey. Beeswax from the honeybee's combs is used in lubricants, salves, ointments, polishes, candles, foods, and dozens of other products.

Indispensable Insects

Insects can be hugely beneficial as biological controllers of plant and animal pests.

Above

Tiny Drosophila melanogaster fruitflies are as important to science as the laboratory rat. They breed easily in bottles on a fruit and yeast mixture, completing their life cycle in a matter of days. They are used to study genes and DNA in breeding experiments.

About 10,000 species of insects can become pests of crop plants (see page 146). They can be controlled by changing farming methods, by treatment with chemical pesticides, or by using their natural predators and parasites, which are often insects themselves. This last method is termed biological control.

Ladybugs and wasps

One of biocontrol's first successes was the cottony-cushion scale insect. About a hundred years ago it was a serious pest of Californian orange tree groves. Then a species of ladybug was deliberately introduced into the orchards, and ate the scale insects almost into oblivion. Other early successes were the greenhouse whitefly, controlled by the parasitic wasp *Encarsia*, and the cabbage white butterfly, controlled in New Zealand by another wasp, *Pteromalus*.

Chemicals take over

From the 1940s, chemical pesticides gradually took over. They were effective (at first), they made farming easier and more efficient, and the chemical companies reaped huge profits.

But pesticides are difficult to target. They kill many insects, pests, and their predators alike. They may get into the soil, water, and food chains, and affect the health of other animals and even people. They have become expensive. And insects, which can evolve so fast, soon become resistant to them.

Back to the roots

Modern experiments with flooded paddy fields of rice crops show that the farmer can improve the "balance sheet" by replacing pesticides with traditional farming methods. The pests' natural predators keep them in check. The farmers no longer pay for expensive insecticides. And they can also catch edible fish in the irrigation channels – fish which formerly had been poisoned by chemical pesticides.

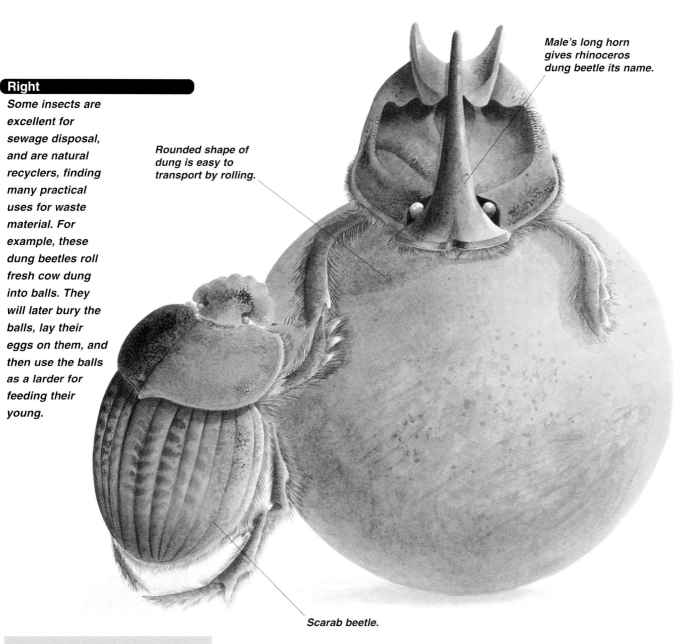

Some insects are excellent for sewage disposal, and are natural recyclers, finding many practical uses for waste material. For example, these dung beetles roll fresh cow dung into balls. They will later bury the balls, lay their eggs on them, and then use the balls as a larder for feeding their young.

Rounded shape of dung is easy to transport by rolling.

Male's long horn gives rhinoceros dung beetle its name.

Scarab beetle.

THE MARCH OF THE PRICKLY PEAR

The prickly-pear cactus was taken to Australia as a hedging and fencing plant, and to produce the dye cochineal. (This is made from the dried, ground-up bodies of the cochineal scale insect that feeds on it.) The newcomer soon caused one of the greatest plant plagues of modern times – but it was stopped by a moth.

1787 Prickly-pear cactus (*Opuntia*) is introduced into Australia, to produce cochineal and as a thorny, protective hedging plant.
1800s The cactus spreads like wildfire across the dry Australian bushland, unchecked by natural herbivores, pests, or parasites.
1920 Almost 1 million hectares of eastern Australia are a thorny wasteland, covered by prickly pear.
1925 2,750 eggs of the moth *Cactoblastis cactorum* are brought from Argentina, and bred.
1928-30 3 billion moth eggs are distributed in prickly-pear areas; they hatch into cactus-eating caterpillars.
1950 Most of Queensland and New South Wales are clear of the prickly pest.

Pest Status

**Most insects have no direct interaction with us.
But some are unquestionably harmful.**

*The skeleton of
an elm tree killed
by Dutch elm
disease. The tree
became infected
by an elm-bark
beetle carrying
the disease.*

Insects do not eat our farm crops and parasitize our farm animals just to annoy us. We come into conflict with them because we create unnatural conditions, with huge fields of the same species of plant, and great herds of the same kind of livestock. The insects respond by taking advantage and breeding in unnaturally high numbers.

In the field

Insects destroy crops in several ways. First, they consume the plants as they grow and ripen in the field, leaving less for us. Grasshoppers, true bugs, aphids, and beetles are the most serious offenders. The Colorado beetle causes periodic famine as it infests fields of potatoes. Giant swarms of locusts strip huge areas of all vegetation. Spruce budworms wreck plantations of spruce and similar timber trees. There are many other examples.

In the store

Secondly, insects can infest stores of grains, cereals, fruits, and other plant harvests. Most of this damage is caused by a few species of beetles, infamously the mealworms, which are the grubs (larvae) of the darkling or hardback beetles (*Tenebrio*).

Third, insects can cause or spread plant diseases. The actual diseases are often due to microbes such as bacteria, viruses, or fungal spores. These get into the plant through holes and wounds where insects feed, bore, or lay eggs.

Eating us out of house and home

Certain insects damage our structures and possessions as well. Throughout the warmer parts of the world, termites threaten wooden structures, from huts to bridges. Carpenter ants and wood-boring beetles pose a similar, but smaller problem.

Silverfish (*Thysanura*) and book lice (*Psocopterans*) destroy books and papers as they feed on paste, glue, and the "size" or coating used for glossy pages. The caterpillars of clothes moths munch on natural fibers in our garments and soft furnishings. Carpet beetles (*Dermestids*) do more of the same type of damage, since they attack both natural and synthetic fibers.

Insects and Human Disease

Millions of people suffer and die from the diseases caused or spread by insects.

Insects spread many diseases in many ways. Biting insects like mosquitoes take germs into their guts when they feed on an infected victim, sucking up blood and body fluids through their hypodermic, needle-like mouth parts. Then they distribute the microbes at every subsequent meal. Before they feed, they use the mouth parts to inject their own fluids (and the microbes), which stop the host's blood from clotting. Different types of mosquitoes transmit malaria, yellow fever, encephalitis, and filariasis (elephantiasis).

Above

Mosquitoes have been responsible for 50 percent of all human deaths.

More culprits

Another well-known bloodsucker is the tsetse fly, which transmits African sleeping sickness (trypanosomiasis) from cattle to humans. New-World sleeping sickness, or Chagas' disease, is carried by certain assassin bugs. Fleas spread bubonic plague; lice can transmit typhus and relapsing fever; and bed bugs are being studied, since they may spread hepatitis.

DISEASES SPREAD BY INSECTS

An animal agent that spreads an infection is called a vector.

Malaria
Cause Protists (one-celled organisms) *Plasmodium*
Vector Female mosquitoes *Anopheles* (the males feed on plant juices)
Affects 400 million people in warmer regions

Filariasis (elephantiasis)
Cause Filarial nematode worms (roundworms)
Vector Various mosquitoes and biting flies
Affects 250 million people, mainly in the tropics

River blindness (onchocerciasis)
Cause Roundworms *Onchocerca*
Vector Blackflies *Simulium*
Affects 40 million people

Sleeping sickness (trypanosomiasis)
Cause Protists *Trypanosoma*
Vector Tsetse flies *Glossina* in Africa, and assassin bugs or "kissing bugs" *Triatoma* in the Americas
Affects 22 million people

Mosquitoes
Blackflies

Yellow fever
Cause Arboviruses
Vector Mosquitoes *Aëdes aegypti*
Affects 45 million people

Leishmaniasis (kala-azar)
Cause Protists *Leishmania*
Vector Sandflies *Phlebotomus*
Affects 12 million people

Tsetse flies

Assassin bugs

Sandflies

Paddling in germs

Another major method of spread is simply by physical contact. Houseflies and other flies paddle and feed in all manner of infected substances, from rotting animals to raw sewage. They then crawl over our bodies, foods, utensils, towels, and kitchen surfaces, transferring the germs that cause cholera, typhoid, dysentery, diarrhea, tuberculosis, anthrax, and many other diseases.

Human problems

Insects are to blame for a vast amount of illness and suffering. But so is the uneven spread of wealth and healthcare around the world. The battles against insects are fought mainly in the warmer, poorer parts of the world, while immunization, drug treatments, and pesticides for wiping out the culprits are expensive, and are made mainly by rich countries, who don't always share these resources with their poorer neighbors.

Would you believe?

The waves of plague of the Middle Ages were caused by bacteria that live in the fleas that live on rats. The 14th-century outbreak was well known as the Black Death. In Europe it killed about 25 million people, a quarter of the population.

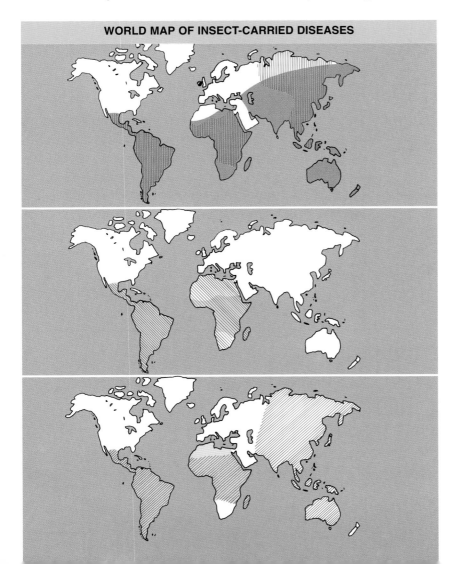

WORLD MAP OF INSECT-CARRIED DISEASES

MALARIA

LEISHMANIASIS

TRYPANOSOMIASIS

YELLOW FEVER

RIVER BLINDNESS

FILARIASIS

Disappearing Insects

Extinctions occur daily in the modern world, and insect species are the main victims.

Above
The world's largest butterfly is Queen Alexandra's birdwing of Papua New Guinea. It is almost extinct, but a few survive in butterfly zoos.

Extinction has always been part of nature. More than 90 percent of all species that ever lived are now extinct. But evolution works gradually, and our modern world changes fast. Many plants and animals cannot keep up. And insects, being so numerous and widespread, bear the brunt of the destruction.

Less habitat
Collectors treasure the dead bodies of rare, selected insects. Farmers use pesticides which kill millions of unselected insects. But the greatest threat, as for most wildlife, is habitat destruction. People take land for roads, farming, houses, and industry. Wetland breeding grounds of dragonflies are drained. Food plants of butterflies are killed by weedkillers. Hedgerows used by nesting bumblebees are grubbed out. Now, thousands of insect species may face extinction, and the number is constantly rising.

COMING AND GOING

- Some 7,000 new species of insects are discovered, described, and officially named every year. This is about 20 per day.
- Before humans changed the world, it's estimated that one species of large animal, like a mammal or reptile, became extinct every 50 to 100 years. This is the natural extinction rate.
- The estimated extinction rate today, for all species large and small, is about 70 per day.

Giant wetas lived in New Zealand for millions of years, safe from predators. Then people arrived, followed by rats, which completely wiped out the wetas from the mainland.

Unknown losses

More than nine-tenths of the world's insect species live in the tropical rainforests – probably. The exact numbers are unknown. So is their disappearance rate. Cutting down just a few trees could cause a rare species to be lost forever. Perhaps half of all tropical insect species may disappear in the next 20 years. We may never know that they existed, and evolution will never replace them.

Would you believe?

• One scientist estimated that 12,000 species live in a hectare of rainforest canopy – and that's just beetles!

• Six-sevenths of these species have never been studied and named.

• Millions of hectares of rainforest are cut down every year.

• There may be anywhere between 5 and 10 million animal species, mostly small insects, still undiscovered in the world.

Glossary

Abdomen The third, rearmost, main part of the insect body. It is divided into up to ten segments. Most of the body's organs, such as guts and reproductive parts, are contained in the abdomen.

Aestivation A period of dormancy when life processes are shut down to a minimum in order to withstand very hot or dry conditions (compare hibernation).

Ametabolous development When the juvenile stages resemble the adult, and there is no dramatic change at maturity.

Antenna (antennae) A pair of sensory appendages on the head of insects and other arthropods, usually long and thin; sometimes called "feelers."

Apodeme An internal attachment for muscles, formed by an ingrowth of the exoskeleton.

Appendages Any parts joined to the main body. Usually refers to legs, antennae, mouth parts, and cerci.

Apterygota A subclass of primitive insects that have never evolved wings. It includes the bristletails and silverfish.

Arachnida A class of arthropods that includes spiders, scorpions, ticks, and mites.

Arthropod An animal with "jointed limbs." The term refers to the phylum that includes insects, arachnids, crustaceans, and myriapods (centipedes and millipedes).

Autoamputation When an animal deliberately breaks off a part of its own body in order to escape from a predator.

Baroreceptors Sensory organs that detect changes in atmospheric pressure or other pressure, such as internal blood or fluid pressure.

Batesian mimicry When a harmless insect (or other animal) mimics a poisonous one in order to avoid being preyed on.

Bombykol The chemical pheromone used by the female silk moth to attract the male.

Camouflage Colors, patterns, and shapes on an animal's body that make it difficult to see against its background.

A lubber grasshopper dispays his antennae or "feelers."

Campodeiform larvae Juvenile or immature forms of an insect species that resemble primitive, wingless insects and have three pairs of walking legs.

Carapace A shell formed from the exoskeleton that covers the back of the thorax and may extend forwards over the head.

Carboniferous Period A geological period between 370 and 280 million years ago.

Carpels The female parts of a flower, consisting of the stigma and style, which receive pollen, and the ovary, which contains the seeds.

Caste A group of insects that perform specific tasks as part of a social system.

Centipedes Segmented arthropods that belong to the superclass Myriapoda and have one pair of legs per segment.

Cephalothorax A part of the body made up of the fused head and thorax.

Cercus (cerci) A pair of sensory appendages located at the end of the abdomen of some insects and other arthropods.

Chemoreceptors Sensory organs that detect chemical stimulation, such as tastes and smells.

Chilopoda The class of arthropods that includes the centipedes.

Chitin A tough carbohydrate (technically, a polysaccharide) that, combined with proteins, forms the exoskeleton of insects.

Chlorophyll The green pigment of plants that enables them to harness the energy of the sun during photosynthesis.

Chordotonal sensilla A rod of cuticle that transmits vibrations from the tympanic membrane of the "ear" of some insects to the sensory nerves.

Chorion The tough, waterproof shell of an insect or similar egg.

Chrysalis The common term for the pupal stage of a butterly or moth, and sometimes for the same stage of a beetle or fly.

Clickbox mechanism An energy storage device, whereby the walls of the thorax spring suddenly from a convex to a concave shape in order to flap an insect's wings.

Cocoon A construction of silk thread wrapped around the pupal stage of some insects; also, a silken container for the eggs of some insects, spiders, and similar animals.

Coleoptera An order of insects that includes all the beetles and weevils.

Compound eyes Light-receptive organs made up of many individual units or ommatidia.

Coxa The uppermost segment of an insect leg, joined to the thorax.

Crustacea The class of arthropods that includes barnacles, crabs, lobsters, prawns, shrimps, and their relatives.

Crypsis Use of camouflage or disguise to hide from predators or prey.

Cuticle The hard, outer layer or exoskeleton of arthropods. It forms a waterproof barrier that functions as a means of support and anchorage for internal body muscles.

Detritivores Animals that consume detritus – waste and dead materials, including feces (droppings) and decaying plant and animal material. Similar to scavengers.

Devonian Period A geological period between 415 and 370 million years ago.

Diplopoda A class of arthropods that includes the millipedes.

Diptera An order of insects that includes the two-winged flies. There are many kinds, such as houseflies, botflies, craneflies, hoverflies, mosquitoes, gnats, and midges. The second pair of wings is reduced to a pair of balancing halteres.

Ecdysin An enzyme that controls molting or shedding of the cuticle in insects.

Echolocation A means of perceiving surroundings by sending out high-pitched sounds and listening for the returning echoes.

Eclosion Emergence of the adult insect from the pupal case.

Ectoparasite An organism that

The green-eyed robber fly has two large, compound eyes for sight.

derives nourishment from another, the host, by feeding on it from the outside, usually by piercing its skin.

Elytra The first pair of beetles' wings, which are thickened to form hard covers for the main body.

Endocuticle The inner layer of cuticle that is mostly reabsorbed prior to molting.

Endoparasite An organism that lives inside another, and uses its host to obtain nourishment and/or shelter.

Endopterygota Advanced insects whose wings develop from internal buds and whose young undergo complete metamorphosis to the adult stage.

Entomology The study of insects.

Epicuticle The outer, waxy, waterproof layer of the cuticle.

Epidermal cell Skin cell.

Epidermis Skin or similar, outermost layer or covering.

Eruciform larvae Juvenile insects that resemble the caterpillars of moths and butterflies, and have three

pairs of thoracic walking legs and several pairs of abdominal prolegs.

Exocuticle The middle layer of the cuticle.

Exopterygota Insects whose wings develop from external buds and whose young undergo incomplete metamorphosis to the adult stage.

Exoskeleton The hard, outer body casing or cuticle of insects that gives structural support and provides a waterproof barrier.

Exuvium The cast skin of an insect after shedding or molting.

Eyespots Insect body patterns that resemble large eyes, usually designed to frighten off a predator.

Facultative parasite An organism that obtains nourishment at the expense of another during part of its development.

Feces Undigested and waste material voided from the anus or digestive tract.

Femur The third segment of the insect leg. It contains most of the leg muscles.

Follicle A small sac, bag or vesicle, usually filled mainly with fluid.

Foregut The front end of the insect alimentary canal or gut, lined by cuticle.

Forelegs The first or front pair of legs, nearest the head end.

Forewings The first or front pair of wings, nearest the head end.

Formic acid A corrosive, stinging liquid with a pungent smell secreted by ants (among others) to deter enemies.

Furcula Part of the spring mechanism of a springtail.

Gall Abnormal growth of plant tissue in response to injury or irritation, often caused by an insect laying eggs in the plant.

Ganglion A wide "lump" of nerves that works as a relay, filtering, and coordination station.

Genital aperture The opening through which the sexual secretions, including eggs and sperm, pass during mating.

Geometrid A family of Lepidoptera,

including the geometer moths, whose caterpillars are known as "loopers" or "inchworms."

Gizzard The part of the alimentary canal or gut where food is ground up.

Guidelines (honey) A pattern of lines on the petals of a flower, thought to guide insects towards the flower's nectaries.

Gyroscope A spinning, balancing device that resists movement and works as a stabilizer.

Habitat The typical place where an organism lives, such as a pond or pine forest.

Habituation When an organism's response behavior changes as a result of continued exposure to a stimulus or situation. It can be confused with learning.

Halteres A pair of balancing organs that have replaced the second pair of wings in dipteran (true, two-winged) flies.

Head The first or foremost part of an animal's body. In most species, including insects, it features sense organs and mouth parts, and contains the brain and the first part of the alimentary canal or gut.

Hemimetabolous development When metamorphosis between the juvenile and adult stages is gradual, and the young insects resemble the adults a little more at each molt.

Hemiptera An order of insects that includes bugs, cicadas, hoppers, aphids, and scale insects. The base of the forewings is often hard.

Hemolymph The blood-like fluid that circulates around an insect's body, carrying nutrients, hormones, and wastes.

Herbivorous Animals that feed on plant parts.

Hermaphrodite An individual having both male and female organs, a condition not found in insects.

Hibernation A period of dormancy when life processes are shut down to a minimum in order to withstand harsh conditions, usually in the winter. (Compare aestivation.)

Hindgut The end part of the alimentary canal, or gut, lined by cuticle.

Hindlegs The last or rearmost pair of legs, furthest from the head end.

Hindwings The second or rear pair of wings, furthest from the head end.

Holometabolous development When metamorphosis or change between the juvenile and adult stage is dramatic, i.e. the young insects are dissimilar to the adults.

Hormones Chemical messengers inside the body produced by hormonal or endocrine glands that travel via the blood stream to control the activities of certain organs and tissues.

Hymenoptera An order of insects that includes the bees, wasps, and ants.

Hypopharynx An extension of the lining of the pharynx, or throat, which serves as a tongue to taste food and guide it down the gullet.

Insecta A class of arthropods that includes segmented animals whose bodies are divided into three parts, and which have six legs and usually two pairs of wings as adults.

Instar A juvenile insect in the immature stage between molts.

Iris cells Cells containing moveable pigments that serve to adjust the amount of light entering the ommatidia of the eye.

Isoptera An order of insects that includes termites.

Insect heads have various shapes, as seen on this green stinkbug.

Jurassic Period A geological period between 210 and 144 million years ago.

Labium A hinged flap or sheath on the head with a pair of sensory palps, which forms a "lower lip" to the mouth.

Labrum A hinged flap or sheath of cuticle on the head that forms the "upper lip" of the mouth.

Larva The juvenile or immature stage of an insect's life, usually not resembling the adult, during which it feeds and grows.

Lepidoptera An order of insects that includes butterflies and moths.

Luciferase The enzyme that carries out the chemical reaction in some insects, resulting in luminescence or the production of glowing light.

Luciferin The chemical involved in the reaction resulting in luminescence.

Maggot The worm-like larval stage of some insects, such as flies.

Malpighian tubules Tiny tubes within the abdomen that function as filters and remove wastes from the blood.

Mandibles A pair of jaw-like pincers, one on each side of the mouth, for cutting and tearing food.

Mantodea An order of insects that includes praying mantises.

Maxillae A second pair of jaw-like appendages with sensory palps, one on either side of the mouth, for holding and tasting food.

Meconium Body wastes that accumulate inside the pupal case during metamorphosis.

Melanic form The black or dark form of an animal.

Melanin A dark pigment of animals.

Mesothorax The middle segment of the thorax.

Metamorphosis The change in body shape and form that insects and other animals, such as amphibians, go through when they pass from the immature form to the adult form.

Metathorax The third or rearmost section of the thorax.

Micropyle The microscopic pore in an egg that allows the entry of sperm for fertilization.

Midgut The middle part of the alimentary canal or gut, unlined by cuticle.

Molting The shedding and regrowth of the cuticle that allows a young insect to grow and develop into an adult.

Mouth parts The appendages at the front of the head and around the mouth, near the front opening of the alimentary canal or gut (digestive tract), which manipulate food.

Müllerian mimicry When several unrelated poisonous or distasteful animals share warning patterns and colors.

Mutations Changes in the genetic code that result in altered characteristics of a living thing, which may be for the better, but are usually detrimental.

Myriapods The superclass of arthropods that includes millipedes and centipedes.

Naiad The aquatic, nymph stage of a dragonfly or damselfly.

Niche The ecological place or role of an organism in nature.

Nymph The larval stage of an exopterygote insect, such as a dragonfly, cockroach, or cricket.

Obligate parasites Animals that take nourishment at the expense of another animal (the host). They cannot survive without the host.

Ocellus (ocelli) A simple eye, with only a single unit of lens and light-sensitive cells.

Odonata An order of insects that includes dragonflies and damselflies.

Olfaction The sense of smell.

Olfactory receptors Sensory organs that detect airborne chemicals or smells.

Ommatidium (ommatidia) A single unit of a compound eye, consisting of lens, light-sensitive cells, and a nerve fiber.

Omnivores Animals that eat both plant and animal parts.

Orthoptera An order of insects that

A bee assassin predator with its deerfly prey.

includes grasshoppers, locusts and crickets.

Oviparous Animals that lay eggs.

Ovipositor The organ used by female insects to position their eggs as they are laid.

Ovoviviparous Animals that incubate the eggs inside their bodies until they hatch, and then give birth to the hatchlings.

Parasite An organism that takes nourishment at the expense of another (the host), but usually does not kill the host.

Parasitoid An organism that takes nourishment at the expense of another (the host), and whose feeding activity usually results in the host's death.

Permian Period A geological period between 280 and 240 million years ago.

Phasmids Stick and leaf insects.

Pheromones Chemical messengers that are volatile and easily released as a "vapor" into the air by an animal, and that affect the behavior of another animal – e.g. attracting a mate, communicating alarm, or initiating dispersal. (*See also* hormone.)

Photogenic organs Organs that produce light.

Phylum (Phyla) A major division in the classification of living things, including those which share basic features – for example, Arthropoda.

Pincers A pair of sharp, pointed appendages that can be moved towards each other in order to hold onto or pierce potential food.

Plecoptera An order of insects that includes the stoneflies.

Pleuron (pleura) The side panels of the segments of the insect body.

Polarized light Light with waves that vibrate in one plane.

Pollination The transfer of pollen from the male parts of flowers to the female parts, so that fertilization can take place and the seeds develop.

Predators Animals that hunt and kill (prey on) other animals for food.

Proboscis Mouth parts that are formed into a sucking or probing tube shape.

Prolegs Leg-like appendages on the rear segments of caterpillars and similar insect larvae that help them to move around. They are not true legs.

Proprioceptors Internal sensory organs that detect the movements and positions of body parts.

Prothorax The first or foremost segment of the thorax, nearest the head.

Pterygota The subclass of higher insects that have evolved wings. It includes all insects other than bristletails and silverfish.

Pulvilli Cushion-like sticky pads on an insect's feet that allow it to cling to smooth surfaces.

Pupa (pupae) An immobile stage during the life of higher insects, between the larval and the adult stages, when complete metamorphosis takes place. Sometimes called a chrysalis.

Puparium (puparia) The last larval skin, which is retained as a shell for the pupa proper in some insects, such as flies.

Retinal cells Cells in the ommatidia of the eye, which contain visual pigments and convert light rays to nerve signals.

Rhabdome Light-sensory structure formed by the inner walls of the ommatidium.

Round dance The circling dance that a returning honeybee scout traces on the side of the comb to indicate to others that food is close to the hive.

Scarabaeiform larvae Juvenile insects resembling the larvae of scarab beetles; they are fat and fleshy, and are usually curled into a 'C' shape.

Scavengers Animals that eat the leftovers of other living things, be it plant, animal, or waste material. Similar to detritivores.

Sclerites Sheets of thick cuticle that form most of the exoskeleton of insects, and are separated by areas of thinner cuticle that allow movement.

Seminal receptacle A sac-like branch of the vagina in female insects, used to store sperm after copulation.

Sensillum (sensilla) A simple sensory organ that detects touch.

Setam (setae) A stiff bristle or hair-like part.

Spermatheca See seminal receptacle.

Spiracles Holes in the cuticle or skin through which air enters and leaves the breathing tubes or tracheae.

Stadium Period between molts.

Stamen The male parts of a flower that have anthers for producing pollen.

Statocyst Sense organ that detects gravity and helps with balance.

Statolith A granule that moves inside a statocyst in response to gravity.

Stereoscopic vision A type of vision that allows the insect to view a scene from two slightly different angles in order to be able to gauge distances.

Sternum The lower or ventral surface of a body segment.

Stridulation When an insect produces sounds by rubbing two specialized body parts together – usually used as part of a courtship ritual to attract a mate.

Stylets Sharp, piercing organs. Some insects have stylets for feeding; others have them for egg-laying.

Symbiosis When two unrelated organisms live together for mutual benefit.

Tactile receptor A sensory organ that detects touch.

Tarsus The "foot" or part of the leg farthest from the body, consisting of up to five segments, the last having a pair of claws.

Tergum The upper or dorsal surface of a body segment.

Tertiary Period A geological period between 65 and 2 million years ago.

Thorax The middle part of the body of an insect. It usually features the legs and wings.

Tibia The fourth segment of the insect leg.

Torpor A period of dormancy when life processes are shut down to a minimum in order to withstand harsh conditions.

Tracheae Breathing tubes for respiration that carry air from the outside into the body tissues.

Tracheole Microscopic branches at the ends of the tracheae.

Trilobites An extinct class of arthropods with many pairs of legs and a carapace divided into three lobes.

Trophallaxis The exchange of food by mouth between members of a social insect colony.

Tymbal A thin skin stretched taut across a space, which is made to vibrate by muscles and so makes sounds.

Tympanic membrane A thin skin stretched taut across a space that is made to vibrate by sounds in the air and so transmits the sounds to nerves – an eardrum.

Vas deferens The tube that carries sperm from the testes to the sperm storage chamber in the male.

Vector An organism that transmits a disease from one host to another.

Velvet worms Soft-bodied, segmented animals belonging to the phylum Onychophora; they may represent an evolutionary link between worms and arthropods.

Venom sac A bladder that stores poisons until required for use.

Ventral nerve cord The main nerve tract along the lower, inner surface of the insect's body.

Vermiform larvae Legless, worm-shaped, juvenile insects.

Viviparous Animals that give birth to live young that have developed inside the mother's body.

Waggle dance The excited dance of a returning honeybee scout, which includes waggling the abdomen on the side of the hive to indicate to others that food is available nearby.

Wing beat The cycle of wing movement as the wing travels up and down.

Wing case The hard, first pair of wings, or elytra, of beetles, covering the second, membranous pair.

The femur and tibia of a locust's leg help it to make its amazingly strong jumps.

Index

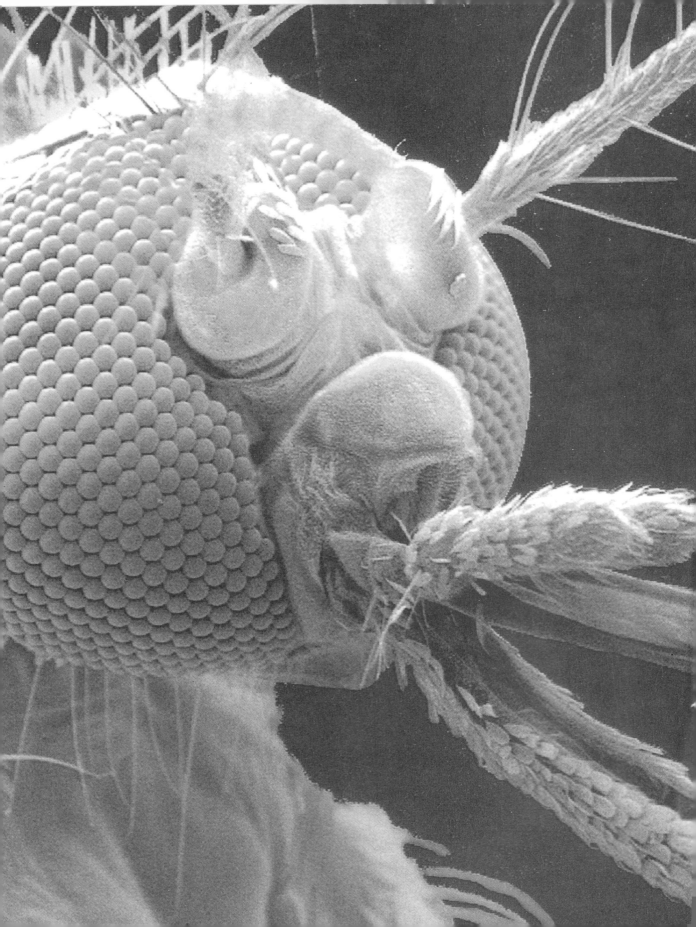